FROM TWO TO FIVE

Kornei Chukovsky

FROM TWO TO FIVE

TRANSLATED AND EDITED BY

Miriam Morton

Foreword by Frances Clarke Sayers

University of California Press

BERKELEY, LOS ANGELES, LONDON

UNIVERSITY OF CALIFORNIA PRESS
BERKELEY AND LOS ANGELES, CALIFORNIA

UNIVERSITY OF CALIFORNIA PRESS, LTD., LONDON, ENGLAND

FIRST PUBLISHED IN RUSSIAN UNDER THE TITLE
ОТ ДВУХ ДО ПЯТИ

THIS TRANSLATION © 1963 BY MIRIAM MORTON
LIBRARY OF CONGRESS CATALOG CARD NUMBER: 63-19028
REVISED EDITION, 1968

Third Printing, 1974

ISBN: 0-520-00237-7 CLOTH
        0-520-00238-5 PAPER

PRINTED IN THE UNITED STATES OF AMERICA

DEDICATED TO GREAT-GRANDDAUGHTER

Mashen'ka

BY HER LOVING GREAT-GRANDFATHER

Foreword

"The Republic of Childhood" was the term used by Paul Hazard in his *Books, Children and Men* (Boston: The Horn Book, Inc., 1944) to describe the reading of children who, generation after generation, acclaim and deeply respond to certain enduring books without regard to the nationality of their origin: *Pinocchio, The Wonderful Adventures of Nils, Robinson Crusoe,* and the rest. There is another world fellowship that deserves equally distinguished recognition: that small commonwealth of those who, having an intuitive kinship with children, fortify and extend it by observation, by scientific and psychological studies, and so increase our sense of wonder and delight in children and cast across the divergent theories of education a long shadow of universal wisdom. The author of this book, Kornei Chukovsky, is such a man: a scholar of adult literatures, as was Paul Hazard of France; a poet of childhood, like the English Walter de la Mare; an observer of children, of their speech and their patterns of learning, as was the Swiss scientist, psychologist, and educator, Jean Piaget.

Chukovsky, the most loved author of books for children in the Soviet Union, received on his eightieth birthday, May 20, 1962, an honorary degree from Oxford University for his "services to British literature in the Soviet Union"—a tribute to his translations of Shakespeare, Swift, G. K. Chesterton, Kipling, and Oscar Wilde. To the writing of books for children he brings the distinctions of translator, editor, critic, and writer, and the perspective of a life that has endured the full drama of the Twentieth Century, lived at the eye of the cyclone. What has such a man to say about the first years of childhood?

That the thought processes of children do not change, only the symbols of their interpretation are adapted to the social structures of their day.

That the child is "armored against thoughts and information that he does not yet need and that are prematurely offered to him by too-hasty adults."

That the young child uses fantasy as a means of learning, and adjusts it to reality in the exact amounts his need demands.

That poetry is the natural language of little children, and nonsense serves as a handle to the proportion of logic in an illogical world.

That the fetish of practicality is a blight upon the literature of childhood. Chukovsky inveighs against those who "look upon every children's book as something that must immediately produce some visible, touchable, beneficial effect, as if a book were a nail or a yoke."

That "the present belongs to the sober, the cautious, the routine-prone, but the future belongs to those who do not rein in their imaginations."

This is a book of immediate and large importance for parents, teachers, and writers of books for children—for everyone concerned with children and the pattern of the future. Moreover, it is a delight to read this skillful and perceptive translation which includes the rendering into English of one of Chukovsky's small, rhymed "epics" of nonsense. It offers, besides its knowledge and insight, the companionship of a wise and loving spirit.

FRANCES CLARKE SAYERS

Translator's Preface

There is a marked divergence these days between the rapidly growing number of translations being published and the very slow
emergence of a recognizable and recognized set of criteria for de-
termining the quality of a translation. Thus, every translator,
especially of literary material, is faced with the problem of the un-
availability of cogent criticism and criteria to guide him. Even as-
suming that he is equipped with a good understanding of the language he translates as well as a creative command of his own, and
is blessed with a sensitive ear for both, he still needs some guidelines
in bridging the gap between the two languages. Lacking these, he
must provide himself largely with his own criteria, and this is a
necessity that inevitably strains his conscience as much as it tires his
brain.

In addition to the standard difficulties of translating from the
Russian (a language certainly not particularly *en rapport* with the
Anglo-Saxon syntax or idiom), rendering *From Two to Five* by
Kornei Chukovsky into English, for American readers, presents a
series of special constraints and obstacles.

Chukovsky is a poet who is extremely painstaking with his prose; his poet's insights, perceptions, and explicit eloquence therefore deserve, in turn, the most painstaking translation. However, all this makes his translator keenly aware of the pitfalls of the art. Furthermore, the author illustrates almost all of his many observations with numerous sayings by young children, with their meaningful and charming distortions of language and reality, but distortions that are extremely difficult to transpose into the vernacular of American children. Fortunately, the basic universality of childhood sense and sensibility has made this challenging task possible, despite occasional approximations. In his own book on translating, *A Noble Art* [*Vysokoe iskusstvo*] (Moscow: Gosudarstvennoe Izdatel'stvo "Khudozhestvennaia Literatura," 1941), Chukovsky has the following to say about a translator's occasional failings:

> The merit or inadequacies of an artistic translation cannot be measured by the presence in it of occasional errors. There are instances when a translator makes dozens of mistakes but, just the same, his translation has great value when it represents a most important quality—the artistic individuality of the translated author as reflected in the uniqueness of his style. . . . The most important thing for the translator to achieve is to re-create in his version of the text the thoughts of the translated author, his "face," his "voice," his literary manner. . . .

It was reassuring to read these words of tolerance!

Owing to its preoccupation with poetry for and by children, *From Two to Five* is replete with samples of verses most of which are rhymed, as they should be, for the young child is virtually addicted to easy rhymes. Of course this presents some soul-trying dilemmas! The translator confesses to having perpetrated several "crimes" to achieve unforced rhyming. The most odious of these was no doubt committed in translating Mayakovsky's folklorish counting rhyme about a boy, Petya, who was five years old (in the Russian version) and his rival who was seven; Petya was made younger by a whole year because four plus seven rhymes with eleven. What boy could forgive such a crime?—especially since his *older* brother remained with his correct age while poor Petya alone was "juvenated."

Before leaving the confessional the translator will admit another offense—this one repeated a number of times—of using "stand-ins" for the purpose of happier rhyming: at times a duck was used in lieu of a hen, a different tree was substituted for the ever-present birch, and so forth. But never—not once—was a verse consciously upgraded or downgraded in rhythm, meaning, or in poetic quality to achieve a more respectable verse translation; such means were definitely considered as not justifying the end.

This being a book about children, and so much of it about their speech and their dialogues with adults, the use of the Russian diminutive is natural, abundant, and enchanting. Even more than usually, therefore, the diminutive, in this instance, was a mixed blessing to the translator. With few exceptions, I was reduced to using the words "little," "tiny," "small," and so forth, to convey the inexpressible (in English) subtle blending of the endearing and the caressing which is contained in diminutive Russian suffixes like -chka, -chkii, -chko, -kaia, -kii, and -koe, and their varied declensions. In fact, the synonym for diminutive (umenshitel'noe) in Russian is laskatel'noe (which means "endearing," "caressing," and "soothing"). In his book on translating, Chukovsky says that the translator must reproduce the smile or the frown contained in the words he translates, not simply the words themselves. But how can one render in another language, especially in English, the little beam of sunshine contained in every Russian laskatel'noe, without writing a whole paragraph or a whole poem for each?

Some of the subject matter of *From Two to Five* makes it advisable to offer not a full but an abridged version in translation. Most of the omissions are from the first chapter, "A Linguistic Genius," a very long chapter which constitutes nearly a third of the entire work. Large sections of it are devoted to a discussion of the Russian child's methods in learning his own language and its intricate syntax and grammar. Of course this material is largely untranslatable, as well as incomprehensible to those who do not know the Russian language. The parts of this chapter which were translated deal with more general and important aspects of the way preschool children acquire the knowledge of their spoken language. There are also sections of this and other chapters which make specific, repeated, or didactic references to Russian folklore. These, too, were omitted because, to appreciate them, the English-speaking reader must be acquainted with the Russian language as well as with its grass-roots origins.

In addition, various passages were omitted because they are repetitive and belabor points that are easy to grasp for American readers, now so accustomed to discussions about children's education, their guidance, and their well-being.

Bracketed material in the text, and the footnotes at the bottom of the page, were supplied by the translator. The author's notes appear at the end of the book.

From Two to Five was first published in the Soviet Union, in 1925, under the title *Little Children (Malen'kie deti)*, and has since been reissued sixteen times. The edition here translated is the thirteenth, published in 1959; 100,000 copies were printed for each of the last three editions. The book was obviously written (this is substantiated by the author in his foreword) not only for specialists but also for the "ordinary" citizen. The "ordinary" Soviet citizen in 1925—and to a considerable extent even his counterpart of more recent years—approached the problems of child rearing, of child education, and of children's literature with a rather untutored and unpracticed mind. The author therefore found it necessary to stress various points with elementary exposition and with marked repetitiveness. In editing this book such passages were shortened or left out to give it greater interest and cohesiveness for the American reader.

The author also found it necessary to reiterate and to state his case at great length in order to overcome the influence of the stubborn socialist-realists who for a long time held a pivotal position in the field of children's education and literature. Such reiteration has been kept to a minimum.

The handicaps of translating and the quandaries of editing this book were not few, but the reasons for rendering it in English far outweighed them in number and importance:

From Two to Five is the only book on the lore of the very young child written by a leading children's poet. It has a distinctive style, it is unique in much of its subject matter, and it is rich in insights of universal application and significance. Kornei Chukovsky is the dean of Russian children's writers. Since the publication in 1916 of his first children's animal tale in verse, *The Crocodile (Krokodil)*, forty million copies of his children's books have been published in the Soviet Union; many of them have been translated into other languages. And not only has this most celebrated Russian children's poet been writing for children for nearly half a century, but he has been, for as long, a keen and analytic observer of the young child, and his loyal and discerning admirer; he has also been a champion of the child's right to grow according to his inherent child's nature, to savor all kinds of experiences and literary fare, and to benefit from the singular educational values of nonsense verse and fairy tales. All this and much more is contained in *From Two to Five*.

In the simultaneous exchange of culture, and invective, between America and the Soviet Union, it is hoped that the translation of this sensitive, instructive, and beguiling book will help tip the scales in favor of culture.

MIRIAM MORTON

From the Author

Those were jolly times—my home was at the edge of the sea and right in front of my windows, on the hot sands, swarmed an infinite number of small children, under the watchful eyes of grandmothers and nurses. The long sandy beach, stretching for almost two kilometers, was virtually seeded with Tanias, Natashas, Vovas, Igors. Sauntering about this beach from morning till dusk, I soon became chummy with this children's world and they, in turn, got used to having me around. Together we built impregnable fortresses of sand and together we dispatched paper fleets into the sea. This went on for ten years.

All around me, without a moment's pause, sounded the melodic speech of children. At first it seemed merely diverting. It took me some time to realize that, not only splendid in itself, this speech also had an intrinsically high instructive value. By studying it, it is possible to discover the whimsical and elusive laws of childhood thinking.

To discover these laws and to formulate them with precision became from those years on my special problem, which I attempt to solve in this book to the best of my ability. This task would be considerably easier if it were not linked with another: to bring my observations not only to the narrow circle of specialists in the psychology of childhood, but also to the masses of readers, and to make this book understandable to every "ordinary" person.

In the first chapter of this book, "A Linguistic Genius," an attempt is made to show, from observation and by means of concrete examples, how vast, varied, and complex is the mental effort that the child from two to five years of age makes in the course of mastering his native tongue. I shall consider my endeavors not futile if I succeed, even only partially, in making the reader share my admiration for those methods, remarkable in their expediency, by which the child, even at the age of two, assimilates the most basic elements of his linguistic culture.

In the chapter, "The Tireless Explorer," I seek to mark the more characteristic of the many processes by which the child becomes aware of the world. This chapter presents the subject at considerably greater length and in greater depth in the present edition than in any of the preceding twelve.

The chapter, "Children and Their Poetry: How Children Make Up Verse," is organically related to the first chapter, for here versification by children is studied as one of the stages in their linguistic development. Although the child does not exist who, between the ages of two and five, does not reveal a predilection for poetry, this area of his intellectual activity and tastes has so far remained unexplored. As I did not have before me an already trodden path, I was obliged not only to gather my own material but also to arrive at my own method of evaluating it. I fear that, as a result of the newness of the study, this chapter is not free of shortcomings. These shortcomings, however, can be obviated only after the poetizing of very young children has become a subject for collective research.

"The Sense of Nonsense Verse" is a chapter dedicated to that very curious genre of children's folk rhymes which, for lack of a ready-made term, I have called "topsy-turvies" [pereviortyshi]. Of course, these topsy-turvies interested me not only in themselves. By making a study of them I sought to prove, in a more concrete and observable manner, that even such deliberate deviations from the realities of life strengthen in children their sense of the real; that along with fairy tales, rhymed topsy-turvies contribute to the education of the young preschool child. The basis of this chapter is the study of children's folklore—Russian and English.

In the chapter, "Conversation with Beginners," I try to share with young poets who are beginning to write for children my extensive experience in writing for the young child. Although this chapter speaks to poets, I hope that it will not be entirely useless to psychologists, educators, parents, and, generally, to everyone who observes and loves children. Needless to say, the rules suggested in this chapter by no means lay claim to being mandatory norms.

Not all, by far, of the children's words and expressions cited in these pages did I hear with my own ears. I treasure a thousand letters in which readers of my newspaper articles and other writings on the language training of young children generously shared with me their own observations of children's speech. Many pages of my book, however, depend on the material which I myself have gathered—*word for word!*—in the course of more than forty years. Nearly every expression has its "passport," for so many came from distant cities and villages across our vast land.

Last year I again turned to my readers to ask them to send me the unusual sayings of their children and of the children of their acquaintances. Letters came in torrents—they enabled me to refurbish my book with many fresh facts relating to the speech of the latest generation of [Russian] children. This abundance of letters is proof that a devoted and, most important, wise love for children has steadily become part of our culture and is widely prevalent.

I warmly thank my reader-friends for their generous help, and appeal to them once more to continue to send me their observations of the life and the speech of children.

The vignettes at the beginning and at the end of chapters are adapted from the motifs of actual children's drawings.

Contents

CHAPTER I

A Linguistic Genius

I Listen . . .

When Lialia was two and a half years old, a man whom she did not know asked her:

"Would you like to be my little daughter?"

She answered haughtily: "I'm only mother's and no other's."

Once when we were taking a walk on the beach, Lialia saw, for the first time, a ship in the distance:

"Mommie, Mommie, the locomotive is taking a bath!" she cried with excitement and amazement.

Enchanting children's speech! It will never cease to give me joy. I once overheard the following delightful dialogue:

"My daddy himself told me this. . . ."

"My mommie herself told me that. . . ."

"But my daddy is himselfer than your mommie—my daddy is much more himself. . . ."

And it cheered me up to hear a three-year-old little girl mutter in her sleep:

"Mom, cover my hind leg!"

Another one, when speaking to her father over the telephone, asked:

"Daddy, why do you have such a dusky-dusky voice today?" This was the first time she had heard her father's telephone voice.

It was a pleasure to find out from kids that a bald man had a barefoot head, that a mint candy made a draft in the mouth, that the husband of a grasshopper was a daddyhopper.

And I would be very amused by such childish expressions and exclamations as:

"Daddy, look how your pants are sulking!"

. . .

"Granny! You are my beloved!"

. . .

"Oh, Mommie! How balloony your legs are!"

. . .

"Our Granny killed the geese in the wintertime so that they would not catch cold."

. . .

"Mommie, I'm so sorry for the baby horses—they cannot pick their noses."

. . .

"Granny, will you die?"

"Yes, I'll die."

"Will they bury you in a hole?"

"Yes, they will bury me."

"Deep?"

"Deep."

"Then, that's when I'll be able to use your sewing machine!"

. . .

George cut a worm in half with his toy spade—

"Why did you do that?"

"The worm was lonesome. Now there are two of them—it is more cheerful for them that way."

. . .

The grandfather admitted that he didn't know how to swaddle an infant—
"Then how did you swaddle Granny when she was little?"

.   .   .

"How dare you pick a fight?" the mother scolded.
"Oh, Mommie, what can I do when the fight just crawls out of me!"

.   .   .

"Once upon a time there was a shepherd. His name was Makar and he had a daughter, Makarona."

.   .   .

"Isn't there something to eat in the cupboard?"
"There's only a small piece of cake, but it's middle-aged."

.   .   .

"Grandpa, the kitty sneezed!"
"Why don't you say 'Good health' [*na zdarov'e*] to the kitty?"
"And who will answer 'Thank you'?"

.   .   .

Philosophy of art: I heard a little boy say: "I sing so much that the room gets big, beautiful. . . ."

.   .   .

"It's so hot in the Crimea! It's like sitting on a primus stove."

.   .   .

"Can't you see? I'm barefoot all over!"

.   .   .

"I'll get up so early that it will still be late."

.   .   .

"Don't put out the light, I can't see how to sleep!"

.   .   .

This child was drawing flowers; around them she drew several dozen dots:
"What are those? Flies?"
"No! They are the fragrance of the flowers."

.   .   .

Liubochka's mother sprayed her with perfume:

"I'm so scenty all over! So perfumey!"

And admiring herself in the mirror, she said, when asked what she was doing:

"I pretty-mire [for "admire"] myself!"

.   .   .

Three-year-old Tania, noticing the lines in her father's forehead, pointed to them with her little finger and said:

"I don't want you to have angry wrinkles [*serditki*]!"

.   .   .

Three-year-old Nata:

"Mommie, sing me a lullaby-ly song!"

Imitation and Creativity

Two- and three-year-old children have such a strong sensitivity to their language—to its many inflections and suffixes—that the words they construct inventively do not seem at all distorted and freakish but, on the contrary, extremely apt, beautiful, and natural.

At times the child creates words that already exist in the language but are unknown to him or to the adults around him. I heard, for instance, a three-year-old child in the Crimea spontaneously use the word "bulleting" [*puliat'*], and he "bulleted" from his tiny rifle all day long, not even suspecting that this word has been thus used for centuries in the faraway Don region. In a story by L. Pantileev, *Len'ka Pantileev*, a Yaroslavl woman says several times: "And so they bullet and they bullet!"

Another child, whose exact age I did not know, created the words "shoeware" [*obutki*] and "clothesware" [*odetki*]; this youngster lived in the steppes near Odessa, not far from the Black Sea. He, too, was completely oblivious of the fact that these two words had existed for a few centuries, in the past, in the distant north, in the Olenets district. How could he possibly have known this since he had not read the ethnographic notes of P. N. Rybnikov [a noted folklorist], who recorded a certain folk tale in which the following words appeared: "I received, as promised, food, shoeware, and clothesware [*obutki i odetki*]." This very same two-part phrase, "shoeware and clothesware," was formulated independently by a small child from the household words for footwear and clothes heard from adults.

"Oh, you grasshopper!" a mother said to her active three-year-old. "I'm not a grasshopper! I'm a 'people' [*liud'*]!"

The mother was nonplused about this "*liud'*," but some time later she discovered, inadvertently, that a thousand kilometers away, in the Urals, a person had been called a *liud'* since the distant past. Indeed, one still says there:

"What kind of a *liud'* is he?"

In this manner the young child at times spontaneously arrives at word structures that were developed by the people over the centuries. His mind masters, as if miraculously, the same methods, processes, and peculiarities of word construction which were used by his very distant ancestors in building the language.

Even the original words invented by children, which do not already exist in the language, seem almost real. They could have come into being, and their absence from the language seems to be merely fortuitous. One somehow reacts to such words as to old acquaintances, feeling that one has already heard them somewhere, at some time.

Having been told by a little boy that a big-horse [*loshada*] "hoofed" [*kopytnula*] him, I used this word [hoofed] at the first opportunity in a conversation with my young daughter. Not only did she understand at once the meaning of the word, but she did not even suspect that it did not exist, for it seemed to her completely normal. And, in a sense, such words *are* normal; at times they are even more "normal" than conventional ones. Why, one might ask, do we call a full-sized horse a "horsie" when speaking to a small child? To a tiny tot a horse must seem enormous. Can we expect him to use a diminutive word for so huge a creature? Sensing the falseness of this diminutive, the child transforms the word "horsie" into "big-horse" [*loshada*], thus underscoring the hugeness of the animal. [The Russian word for an average-sized horse is *loshad'*].

I have heard children deal similarly with other words, using the special word that stands for an unusually large object or animal. In all such instances the child has done exactly what the poet Mayakovsky did when he changed the word "puppy" [*schenok*] into "big-pup" [*schen*]:

> With all his big-pup's might
> The poor creature yelped.
>
> [*Izo vsekh shcheniachikh sil
> Nishchii shchen zagolosil.*]

Changing words, the child most often does not notice his own originality, and thinks that he is repeating words he has heard spoken.

This unconscious word creation first came to my attention, and amazed me, when a four-year-old boy, whose acquaintance I had just made on the train, kept insisting that I let him touch a certain gadget I was holding in my hand. He invented a word for this object, right there and then, and this revealed an extraordinary skill in adapting a suffix that often appears at the end of Russian words to denote the instrumentality of an object—the "l" suffix. An example of this "l" suffix is the way the word *myt'*, which means "to wash," is converted to *mylo*, which means "soap"; the "l" in the word *mylo* is the suffix of instrumentality. This process of distinguishing and classifying, and then using, a certain suffix so aptly seemed to me so impressive because the child, at his young age, was still totally unaware of his inventiveness in this respect.

One notices the same grammatical skill [in young preschool children] in their use of grammatical forms; a child having no notion of grammatical rules uses quite correctly all noun cases, verb tenses, and moods, even when he uses unfamiliar words. This perceptive use of words is a most amazing phenomenon of early childhood!

Even the mistakes that the child often makes in the process of this creative mastering of speech are evidence of the tremendous achievement of his mind in coördinating bits of linguistic knowledge. For instance, although a child could not explain why he calls a letter carrier a "mail*er*" [i.e., calls a *pochtal'on* a *pochtanik*], this reconstruction of the word is evidence that he has become aware of the use of the suffix ["-er" in English] *-nik* in the Russian language, which characterizes a person according to his work or trade. Adults may laugh at "mailer" or *pochtanik* [*pochta* means "mail" in Russian], but it is not the child's fault that etymology does not adhere to a strict logic. If words came into existence according to a consistent principle, children's locutions would not seem so diverting; they are often more "correct" than grammar and "improve" upon it.

To be sure, in order to learn the language, the child imitates adults in his word creativity. It would be nonsense to claim that he *adds* to a language in any way. Without suspecting it himself, he directs all his efforts, by means of analogies, toward assimilating the linguistic riches gradually developed by many generations of adults. But the young child adapts these analogies with such skill, with such sensitivity to the meaning and significance of the elements from which words are formed, that it is impossible not to be enthralled by the power of his understanding, awareness, and memory, so apparent in the very arduous effort he makes every time he speaks.

The minutest variation in grammatical form is apprehended by the child, and, when he needs to contrive (or re-create in his memory) one word or another, he applies precisely that suffix or precisely that grammatical word ending which, according to the mysterious laws of his native tongue, is essential for the needed nuance or meaning or image.

A two-year-old girl was taking a bath and making her doll "dive" into the water and "dive out" of it, commenting:

"There, she drowns-in—now, she drowns-out!" [*"Vot pritonula, vot vytonula!"*]

Only a deaf-mute would not notice the exquisite plasticity and the refined meaning of these words. "Drowns-in" is not the same thing as "drowns"—it is to drown only temporarily with a definite expectation implied that the doll would be "drowning-out" again. . . .

It seems to me that, beginning with the age of two, every child becomes for a short period of time a linguistic genius. Later, beginning with the age of five to six, this talent begins to fade. There is no trace left in the eight-year-old of this creativity with words, since the need for it has passed; by this age the child already has fully mastered the basic principles of his native language. If his former talent for word invention and construction had not abandoned him, he would, even by the age of ten, eclipse any of us with his suppleness and brilliance of speech. Not in vain did Leo Tolstoy, addressing himself to adults, write: ". . . [the child] realizes the laws of word formation better than you because no one so often thinks up new words as children." [1]

Of course, when we speak of the creative powers of the young child, of his keen sensitivity to language, of his genius, we do not consider these words sentimental hyperboles. But we must not, just

ZAKALIAKA

[A drawing by a little girl who created the word "Zakaliaka" (derivative from the Russian word for "doodle") to describe what she drew. Chukovsky wrote a children's poem about this drawing and the way it frightened the "artist."]

the same, forget that the basis for all the linguistic aptitude attributed to the child "from two to five" is imitation, since every new word he invents he creates in accordance with the norms made known to him through adult speech. However, he does not copy adults as simply (and as docilely) as it seems to the casual observer. In another section of this chapter, "Children as 'Critics' of Adult Speech," a large amount of evidence is presented to show that in the process of assimilating his native spoken language the child, from the early age of two, introduces a critical evaluation, analysis, and control.

The young child acquires his linguistic and thinking habits only through communication with other human beings. It is only this association that makes a human being out of him, that is, a speaking and thinking being. But, if this communication with other human beings did not evoke in him, for even a short period of time, a special, heightened sensitivity to the materials of speech which adults share with him, he would remain, to the end of his days, a foreigner in the realm of his own language—as though repeating lifelessly the dull rules of textbooks.

In the old days I had occasion to meet children on whom were imposed, from a very early age and for various reasons (mainly because of the [snobbish] whims of rich and shallow parents), the vocabulary and the structure of a foreign language, most often French. These unfortunate children, estranged from the elements of their native speech, mastered neither their own nor the foreign language. Their speech, in both instances, was equally colorless, bloodless, and pallid, because, during the age "from two to five" they were deprived of the possibility of familiarizing themselves creatively with their spoken language.

To be sure, many neologisms of the child are often evidence of his inability to make himself conversant, in his early attempts to speak the language, with this or that exception to a grammatical norm. At times a word or a locution "invented" by the child, which seems to us so original, has occurred to him actually only because he has applied to it, too directly, some [grammatical] rule, unaware of any exception to it. Despite this, I am convinced of the tremendous speech-giftedness of the preschool child.

This giftedness consists not only in his early ability to classify word

endings, prefixes, and suffixes, a process he accomplishes unconsciously in his two-year-old mind, but also in the divination with
which he chooses them when he creates a new word, imitating and
using for such a word an appropriate model. Imitation itself is in
this way a creative act.

It is frightening to think what an enormous number of grammatical forms are poured over the poor head of the young child. And
he, as if it were nothing at all, adjusts to all this chaos, constantly
sorting out into rubrics the disorderly elements of the words he hears,
without noticing, as he does this, his gigantic effort. If an adult had
to master so many grammatical rules within so short a time, his head
would surely burst—a mass of rules mastered so lightly and so freely
by the two-year-old "linguist." The labor he thus performs at this age
is astonishing enough, but even more amazing and unparalleled is
the ease with which he does it.

In truth, the young child is the hardest mental toiler on our planet.
Fortunately, he does not even suspect this.

We have said earlier that by the time the child reaches his eighth
year his keen sensitivity to his language is dulled. However, it does
not follow that his linguistic development suffers to any extent from
this loss. Having lost his recent giftedness to improvise original word
structures, he replaces this lack a hundredfold with valuable new
qualities of his linguistic growth. The linguistic work of the child
has now switched to new rails. Using his achievements of the earlier
period, he now equips himself for more intricate and varied communication with others.

"At this age," says A. N. Gvozdev,[2] "the child has already mastered
to such a degree the entire complicated grammatical system, including the finest points of the esoteric syntactic and morphological
sequences in the Russian language, as well as the solid and correct
usage of the many single exceptions, that the Russian language, thus
mastered, becomes indeed his own." All this becomes obvious to
those who, for instance, study with sufficient awareness the intellectual endeavors of school children who were only recently preschoolers. The fact remains incontrovertible, however, that the
process of learning one's native language has a much faster tempo
specifically at the age of "from two to five."

It has been established for a long time that at the age of about one
year the child knows less than ten words; at the end of two years his

vocabulary has grown to 250 or 300 words, and by the end of his third year it is in the thousands—that is, in only a year's time the child builds up his basic word "reservoir," and after this accumulation of new words proceeds much more slowly.[3] The same is true of the grammatical forms that the child learns in the same period. I once tried to make a list of these forms (declensions, conjugations, the use of prefixes and suffixes). I noted down not less than seventy. Most of these "generalizations" that are formed in the child's brain forever, for his entire life, are established between the ages of three and four, when the linguistic giftedness seems to be particularly strong.

Children as "Critics" of Adult Speech

Unfortunately, we are not yet rid of those "theoreticians" who continue to maintain that in respect to language the child is a mere automaton who imitates adult speech without discrimination or analysis. This notion is declared [dogmatically] even in learned articles—it is thus "declared" precisely because it cannot be proved. One need only observe closely the speech of young children to notice that they imitate at the same time as they examine and analyze. Is there a child who has reached his fifth year without having repeatedly bothered his mother with questions that revealed his strict and even disparaging criticism of the way adults use certain words and expressions?

"Why do you say penknife? It should be pencil-knife," a little boy objected.

When their grandmother said that winter was coming soon, her grandchildren laughed and wanted to know:

"Do you mean that winter has legs?"

The logic of four-year-old rationalists is merciless. They admit no exceptions. Every liberty taken with words seems to them arbitrary. One might say in conversation, for instance:

"I'm dying to hear that concert!"

"Then why don't you die?" a child would ask sarcastically.

A saleswoman said one day after returning home from her job:

"The devil only knows what goes on in our store."

"Well, what goes on there?" her husband asked.

Their five-year-old son objected to the question and remarked instructively:

"She just said that the devil only knows. Is mama a devil? She doesn't know!"

The fact is that adults think in terms of allegories and metaphors, whereas children think in terms of objects perceived in their world of objects. Their thinking is limited during the first years to images of things; this is why they object so strongly to our symbolism.

A woman, for example, asked her four-year-old Natasha:

"Tell me, what does it mean to say that a person is trying to drown another in a spoonful of water [a Russian expression]?"

"What did you say? In what kind of spoon? Say that again."

The mother repeated the adage.

"That's impossible!" Natasha said categorically. "It can never happen!"

Right there and then she demonstrated the physical impossibility of such an act; she grabbed a spoon and quickly placed it on the floor.

"Look, here am I," and she stood on the spoon. "All right, drown me. There isn't enough room for a whole person—all of him will remain on top. . . . Look for yourself . . . the foot is much larger than the spoon!"

And Natasha expressed scorn for such an absurd idea conceived by grownups, saying:

"Let's not talk about it any more—it's such nonsense."

Other children, endowed with a sense of humor, often pretend that they cannot understand this or that adult idiom and try to "train" us to observe more closely the rules that we ourselves have taught them. If you complain in the presence of a child that your head is splitting, he might say:

"Then why can't I hear it split?"—he would thus underscore his negative attitude to the odd way adults express their thoughts metaphorically, a way so unlike the obvious.

After a long separation, a mother said to her little girl:

"How thin you've become, Nadiusha. All that's left of you is one little nose."

"Well, Mommie, did I have more than one nose before you left?"

When a child heard that a woman "fell into a faint," she asked, with a noticeable twinkle in her eye:

"Who dragged her out of it?"

Her father said to Maniusha: "Come on, skate out of my room!

I have work to do." ["Skate out" is a politer, Russian way of saying "Scram!"]

"I'll not skate out—I have no roller skates."

Playing with his son's toy soldiers, the father suggested that one of them would stand watch. The boy picked up the toy soldier and, laughing, ran to the wall clock to place it there, knowing quite well what "stand watch" meant.

However, these polemics with adult speech are not always carried on in jest. I know a four-year-old child who gets furious whenever she hears an adult speak about ladyfinger biscuits:

"They are not made out of fingers, they're made out of dough!"

Most often the criticism is caused by the child's confusion about the way adults use words. The child whom we ourselves have trained to see sense in every word cannot forgive us the "senselessness" that we introduce into some of our expressions. It is difficult for the pre-school child to understand even simple idioms and figurative expressions.

"I'll never go to school," five-year-old Seriozha announced. "They cut [flunk] children there."

A visitor asked about his baby sister: "Does your little Irishka go to sleep with the roosters?"

"No, she doesn't go to bed with the roosters. They scratch! She sleeps in her cradle."

At times this childish inability to understand figurative expressions causes adults considerable embarrassment.

Four-year-old Olia, who came with her mother to visit a Moscow aunt, looked closely at this aunt and her husband as they were all having tea, and soon remarked with obvious disappointment:

"Mama! You said that uncle always sits on Aunt Aniuta's neck but he has been sitting on a chair all the time that we've been here."

I am sorry, but I cannot repeat what the mother said in reply.

This reminds me of an incident in an American family:

"Betty, why didn't you provide a knife and fork for Mr. White?"

"Because I thought he didn't need them—daddy said he ate like a horse."

An exasperated mother said to her son: "Some day you'll lose your head, so help me God!"

"I'll never lose *my* head," was the reassuring reply, "I'll find it and pick it up."

The child reacts with such innocence to idioms because he takes them literally.

A critical attitude toward the meaning and the use of words is observable not only in gifted children but in almost all children. And the same criticisms and objections and the same word adaptations and word inventions recur among children in different geographic regions and in different generations.

Camouflaging Ignorance

Everyone remembers the eloquent lines Leo Tolstoy wrote about the first years of his life:

"Was it not then that I acquired all that now sustains me? And I gained so much and so quickly that during the rest of my life I did not acquire a hundredth part of it. From myself as a five-year-old to myself as I now am there is only one step. The distance between myself as an infant and myself at five years is tremendous."[4]

Among the early acquisitions of the child's mind, the one having the highest value is his treasure of words and grammar. He himself hardly notices the gigantic effort he is exerting while he accomplishes this learning so systematically, expediently, and expeditiously. Nevertheless, an irreproachably correct mastering of speech is for many children a great ambition and joy. I am sorry to say that I do not have in my possession enough material to give me the right to maintain that this noble ambition, based on an avid urge for intellectual accomplishment, is characteristic of all children. Even the partial evidence I have managed to gather, however, confirms the belief that this feeling is widespread among children "from two to five."

I first came across an amazing example of it when Yurik, two and a half years old, once made a slip of the tongue and said instead of "screw"—"shew." When corrected, he said unabashedly:

"Boria said 'shew' but Yurik said 'screw.' "

This Yurik did not number among his acquaintances a single Boria. He invented a Boria for the express purpose of pinning on him all his mistakes and blunders, crediting himself only with faultless speech. "It's Boria who said *mamovar;* Yurik always says *samovar.*" Inventing the scapegoat, Boria, the shrewd tot assured for himself complete peace of soul. Thanks to this imaginary Boria, he himself remained, under all circumstances, an infallible authority on spoken Russian, enjoying, in addition, the satisfaction of ridiculing a defeated "competitor." By means of this machination, a two-and-half-year-old child shielded his sensitive ego—he had found his mistakes so embarrassing that he had to invent a double to burden with his own mistakes.

The more I looked into this matter, the more was I convinced that Yurik was not an exception but the rule. The French novelist, Georges Duhamel, tells a similar story about a three-year-old Parisienne. He wrote: "She was terribly mischievous, cunning and resourceful. She experimented with adult speech and, to avoid responsibility, she blamed all her errors on an imaginary brother." This is exactly what Yurik did.

A mother wrote me about a similar device used by her three-year-old Clara:

"She made a mistake and called a comforter a 'compoter.' Everyone laughed. Clara then began to laugh with the others and said: 'That Lialia, she is such an odd one—everyone says "comforter" but she says "compoter." ' Lialia was her younger sister."

Linguistic "ego satisfaction" plays an important part in the child's mental development. It is very useful to him in the course of mastering his spoken language. In the process of transposing his mistakes to an imaginary dunce, he learns the correct word so well that he will never again make the same mistake—the correct word has thus made a lasting impression on his mind. This most inquisitive of all creatures, the child "from two to five," values knowledge above all else.

This artless cunning, to camouflage ignorance or phonetic incompetence, is also found in children's poetry. In one of her poems, Agnia Barto tells of a little boy who could not pronounce the letter "r" and would say "Malina" [raspberry] instead of the name "Marina." His mother tried to teach him to pronounce this letter:

> She repeats: "Say 'metro'—try!
> By metro we'll go to Uncle Gus."
> "No," he says, for he's sly—
> "Let's go today by bus."

While taking a walk with his aunt, a two-year-old boy stopped at a bookstall. The vendor asked him:

"Can you read?"

"Yes, I can."

He gave him a book and invited him to read. Imitating his aunt, the boy felt in his pocket and said:

"I forgot my glasses at home."

The child would not resort to such tricks of diplomacy if his awareness of his incompetence did not cause him so much distress. No matter what, he wants to consider himself capable and informed. Evidently such self-deception is, for the time being, necessary for the child. I have noticed that even the most bashful and modest people were show-offs and braggarts in their childhood. The instinct of self-assertion is usually quite strong at this age. Particularly is this self-assertion expressed in relation to skill and knowledge. And isn't it for the same reason that the child gloats so loudly when he succeeds in catching an adult in making the least mistake in speech?

Teaching the Child Proper Speech

When we are so delighted with those marvelous methods by which the young child learns how to speak his native tongue, should we overlook the fact that, as adults, we have the obligation to train him to speak correctly? And when we admire the ingenuity with which the child adapts and invents words, do we have the right to let him cultivate them in his speech? It would be a crying shame if we did either. Although no one can take away our right to be charmed by the linguistic creativity of the young child, we would violate the most elementary principle of education if we decided to praise, in his presence, this or that word invented by him, and if we tried, for the sake of originality, to retain such a word in his vocabulary. No matter how much we admire the child's word creations, we must tell him:

"We don't say it this way. You should say thus and so."

Much work in training the preschool child to speak well is done in our kindergartens. One may acquaint oneself with the methods of this work through the various articles published during the past few years by the Academy of Pedagogic Sciences and by the Ministry of Education, U.S.S.R.[5]

The main task in this education is to train the child to come ever closer to good adult speech. It must be pointed out to those doting parents who enjoy with a gourmet's relish the whimsical vocabulary of children and who preserve it in their speech for their own delectation, that doing this will retard the child's linguistic development. There are mothers, grandmothers, and grandfathers who are so enraptured by the cute sayings of a beloved youngster that they even forget to be offended when such a youngster expresses a lack of respect for them by means of verbal cuteness.

Ira, five years old, for some reason started to pick on her grandfather:

"What do you have in your head? Straw? If it's a brain that you have, it isn't very 'decisioned' [*nedodumchivye*]."

And the grandfather, instead of making his granddaughter feel ashamed of herself, started to praise aloud, and in her presence, the invented word. And thus he proved that his brain had, indeed, the characteristic that Ira ascribed to it.

To smack one's lips in the presence of the child at the delicious words he creates at ages "from two to five" encourages in him conceit and self-adulation. But it does not at all follow that adults have the right to interfere despotically with the process of the child's word inventiveness. While correcting their mistakes, we must not block off from them that natural road on which they proceed, in every generation, to the final goal of mastering their native language.

We must not forget also that part of our task in helping the child acquire a knowledge of his spoken language is the constant enrichment of his speech with more and more new words. Since a child's mental growth is closely connected with the growth of his vocabulary, it is easy to see how important this task is. In this sense, to teach a child to speak well means also to teach him to think well. One is inseparable from the other.

Children are trained in all Soviet kindergartens to narrate, and special care is taken in training them to narrate coherently. All this is, of course, splendid—but only when the educator is endowed with good pedagogic sense. If he is too exacting with his constant corrections, he represses the child's free expression of his feelings and ideas and does not leave room for his emotional and mental gropings. He thus risks fading the color out of the child's speech, making it anemic and devitalized, killing in it its wonderful childishness and inflicting a permanent harm. Rigid methods are not desirable here; excessive zeal will prove harmful. Good results can be obtained only by teachers who will act indirectly, with restraint, not too persistently— almost imperceptibly.

After the child achieves correct speech to a sufficient degree, he will have to do a great deal of difficult mental work before his flexible and receptive mind will orient him properly to the surrounding world.

About this—in the following pages.

CHAPTER II

The Tireless Explorer

There is nothing in the reasoning process except associations—
there is thus nothing but correct and incorrect associations. . . .

I. P. PAVLOV *

His Search for Certainty

To those who express an absurd opinion we often say, with scorn or
indignation:

"You are using a child's logic! You reason like a child!"

To most of us this accusation seems both justifiable and just; indeed, we often hear from small children the most absurd judgments
and deductions.

However, we need only think deeper about these "absurdities"
of the very young to be forced to reject this hasty opinion; we would
then understand that in these absurdities is reflected a burning need

---

* I. P. Pavlov (1849–1936), the world-famous experimental psychologist, was
renowned for his discovery of the conditioned reflex.

for the young mind, no matter how, to take measure of the world and to search out, among the many separate aspects of existence, those elements of coherence whose presence the child strives to find from a very early age.

The following incident occurred at a summer place near Leningrad. A mad dog happened to be shot just at the time when the sun was setting in a flame-red aura; from that day on two-and-a-half-year-old Maia would say, every time she saw a red sky at sundown—

"Again they killed a mad dog!"

It is easy to scoff at this immature thinker who imagined that because of some dying dog the heavens were set afire! But has not this child thus expressed the priceless urge to establish the causal connection between separate facts which constitutes the moving force of all man-created sciences?

This urge frequently leads the child to the most fantastic deductions. This, for instance, was the way four-year-old Tasia mastered the word "trained." She came into contact with this word for the first time in the circus, where she saw an act by trained dogs. As a result, when six months later she heard that the father of one of her little friends was "well trained," she asked, with happy anticipation:

"That means that Kirochka's daddy is—a dog!"

This mistake is, again, quite a "respectable" one; it expresses a splendid ability of the young human mind to adapt to every new complex of unfamiliar phenomena, the results of experience attained in other spheres.

The experience of the young child is inevitably very limited, and for this reason he applies it at times inappropriately.

A train ran over a pig, maimed and killed it. Five-year-old city-bred Zoria witnessed the accident on her vacation in the country. She shed many tears of grief over the unfortunate animal. A few days later she met a frisky live pig.

"The pig glued herself up again," Zoria exclaimed ecstatically.

To such extreme degrees is the child often ignorant of the simplest things he encounters! A newcomer in the world, he meets a dilemma at every step he takes, piling up error upon error.

At the age of two to three every youngster makes an infinite number of similar mistakes based on the deepest ignorance of the most elementary objects and facts.

"Mother, who was born first, you or I?"

.   .   .

"Daddy, when you were little, were you a boy or a girl?"

.   .   .

"I like snow better than sun. I can build a fort out of snow but what can I make out of sun?"

.   .   .

"Put your glasses on or you'll catch cold."

.   .   .

"I like garlic, it smells like sausage."

.   .   .

"Mommie, the nettle bites me?"
"Well, in a way . . ."
"Then why doesn't it bark too?"

.   .   .

"Why do they put a pit in every cherry? We have to throw the pit away anyway."

.   .   .

"The sea has one shore but the river has two."

.   .   .

"The sun sets in the sea. Why is there no vapor?"

.   .   .

"Oh, the moon flew along when we went on the trolley and on the train. She, too, wanted to see the Caucasus!"

.   .   .

"The ostrich is a giraffe-bird."

.   .   .

"A turkey is a duck with a bow around its neck."

.   .   .

Little Olia was feeding bits of cabbage leaves to the chickens:
    "Chickens don't eat cabbage," her mother informed her.
    "I'm giving it to them so that they may save it for after they become rabbits."

.   .   .

"What is a knife—the fork's husband?"

.   .   .

"Daddy, please cut down this pine tree—it makes the wind. After you cut it down the weather will be nice and mother will let me go for a walk."

.   .   .

Liosha buried a meat bone under his window and watered the spot regularly, to grow a cow. Every morning he ran out to see if the cow's horns had yet sprouted. Valen'ka, observing how her mother watered the flowers, began to water her favorite puppy so that he would grow up sooner.

And I found this in my diary about my little daughter, three and a half:

> Mura took off her slipper,
> Planted it in the garden—
> "Grow, grow, my little slipper,
> Grow, little one!
> I'll water you every day
> And a tree will grow
> A miracle tree!
>
> "Barefoot children
> To the miracle tree
> Will hop and skip,
> Pretty red booties
> They will pick
> Saying:
> 'Oh, you, Murochka,
> Oh, you clever one!' "

.   .   .

The sun and the stars are created in a flash in the child's mind, out of the small fire in the hearth:

"Make a fire, daddy, so that it can fly up into the sky and make the sun and the stars."

.   .   .

I knew a little boy who would often question his mother about where the night went in the morning. Once, coming across a deep ditch whose bottom was dark, he whispered:

"Now I know where the night hides itself."

. . .

And here is a reason for the arrival of spring:
"The winter got so cold it ran away somewhere."

. . .

A child from the north trying to fall asleep the first evening of his vacation in southern Crimea:
"Mommie, turn off the sun."

. . .

Marina said to her mother one morning:
"Mother, why don't you ever appear in my dreams?"
And in the evening of the same day she said:
"Lie down on my pillow, mommie, we'll look at my dream together."

. . .

Once when two-year-old Eli felt offended, he threatened:
"I'll make it dark, at once." And, closing his eyes, he was convinced that, as a result, the entire world was plunged into darkness.

In every sentence just quoted, in every childish act, is revealed complete ignorance of the simplest things. Of course, I cite these expressions not to scorn childish absurdities. On the contrary, they inspire me with respect because they are evidence of the gigantic work that goes on in the child's mind which, by the age of seven, results in the conquest of this mental chaos. It is impossible not to be amazed at the brevity of the time during which the child acquires such vast riches of varied knowledge. By the time he enters grade school he is no longer lost in the delusions that were typical of his years "from two to five." By this time his "erudition" is so vast, he is so marvelously well oriented to the world of objects and facts, that he will never again utter any of the phrases quoted in the beginning of this chapter. He knows definitely that chickens do not grow into rabbits, that the fork is not married to the knife. The enormous difference we notice between the scope of knowledge of the young preschool child and of the young school child tells us about the miracle-performing mental activity during this early period of the child's existence.

Here are a few examples of the great lack of knowledge in the young preschoolers regarding anatomy, physiology, and so forth:

A naked little boy stands in front of the mirror and says thoughtfully:

"Eyes are for seeing . . . ears are for hearing . . . the mouth for talking . . . and the navel? . . . is for what? Must be for beauty. . . ."

.   .   .

The mother was nursing her newborn daughter. Her five-year-old son observed her closely and asked with utter seriousness:

"Mommie, do you have coffee there sometimes too?"

.   .   .

"Isn't it wonderful! I drink coffee, water, tea, cocoa, but out of me pours only tea."

.   .   .

The grandmother had just removed her artificial teeth. Yurochka burst into peals of laughter and said:

"Now take out your little eyes, Granny."

No matter how many childish mistakes we quote, it is impossible not to be enraptured by the apparently stubborn determination of the child to bring at least illusory order into his limited and fragmentary knowledge of the world. Let the child at first establish associations in a haphazard and spontaneous way; let him apply false analogies. Just the same, the desire to answer for himself the questions—What for? Why? In what way?—is a most important aspect of his psychological development. This search for causal relationships is the basis of culture; it is the guarantee of the progress of human thought. And no matter how often the child stumbles when he takes his first intellectual steps (and he stumbles literally at every such step!), he is following the right road.

Each of these childish judgments which we have just recorded is based either on association through simultaneity or on association through resemblance.

The association through simultaneity was applied, for instance, by two-year-old Maia, the child about whom we spoke at the very beginning of this chapter. She was strongly impressed by two facts which, by coincidence, were simultaneous in time—the sunset, resplendent with flaming colors, which she had never seen before, and the witnessed shooting of the mad dog. Precisely because these two facts were so unexpected, so new and vivid, she isolated them from other facts and at once established between them a causal connection, deciding that dogs are always killed when the sky becomes crimson at sunset. It is not important that on this occasion she was mistaken; I repeat, what *is* important is that on this occasion she revealed the most significant propensity of the human mind to search out the interdependence of observed facts.

Here, so to speak, is the embryo of the cause-and-effect thinking unique to and characteristic of all humanity. Needless to say, it is the duty of adults to point out to the child his errors in an instructive way; but we must not be blind to those delightful methods and processes of reasoning with which the child operates even when he arrives at wrong conclusions. Mistakes will very soon be corrected by experience, accustoming the young one, forever after, to the cause-and-effect explanation of phenomena.

The next step along this road is association through resemblance (or contrast) of objects. A noticeable example of such an association is the observation made by a three-year-old child with regard to the turkey: "A turkey is a duck with a bow around its neck." The child applies one bit of knowledge randomly to another object, and this is his error; but his very attempt to classify objects of the material world according to visible and generic traits, and compare them with other objects, is a hopeful foundation for all his future mental activities.

One Hundred Thousand Why's

But, of course, a child is a child, and not a learned pedant. Despite his tremendous intellectual efforts he never feels like a mental toiler, tirelessly in quest of the truth. Now he plays, now he jumps, or he sings, or he fights, helps his grandmother or his mother with the housework, or he frets, maybe he draws, or listens to a fairy tale; in any event, the interpretation of the life around him is never undertaken by him as a special task of his existence. He never isolates thinking from the rest of his activities, and the very process of his thinking during this period is erratic, sporadic, and easily distracted by other preoccupations. A prolonged concentration of thought is not natural in the preschool child.

It often happens that, posing one or another hypothesis for a puzzling fact, the child forgets it within a minute and improvises a new one. Gradually, he finally works his way toward a more correct understanding of reality, but, of course, one cannot expect that a mistaken hypothesis will always be followed by a more correct one. The child advances toward the truth in wide zigzags.

At times two completely opposite conceptions coexist peacefully in his mind. This is illustrated in the following amazing sentence uttered by a four-year-old girl, a Muscovite:

"There is a God; but, of course, I don't believe in him."

Her grandmother indoctrinated her with the dogmas of orthodox faith, and her father, on the contrary, drew her toward atheism; she, however, wanting to please both, expressed simultaneously, in one short phrase, both faith and disbelief in God, revealing great adaptability and (in this instance) very little concern with the truth:

"There is a God; but, of course, I don't believe in him."

Making two assertions, mutually exclusive, the child did not even notice that the result was an absurdity.

The preschool child has no need at his age for certain truths either on the sociological or on the biological plane; for this reason he plays lightly with concepts, creating for himself, with ease, various fictions and making use of them this way or that, according to his whim.

A four-year-old girl, playing with her wooden horse as with a doll, whispered:

"The horsie put on a tail and went for a walk."

Her mother interrupted her play, saying: "Horses' tails are not tied to them—they cannot be put on and taken off."

"How silly you are, Mommie! I am just playing!"

The truth was that the inseparability of horses from their tails had long been known to the little girl, but, precisely because of this, she could use a contrary notion, creating an imaginary situation, and could play with her toy horse as with a doll—that is, dress and undress it. The more closely I observe children, the clearer it becomes to me that the attitude of our "adults" to the truth often seems strange to the child—especially while he is at play.

What games do not captivate children! Among them imaginary games are great favorites; the usefulness of these is quite obvious— the child seems to be training himself through them for his future mental activities. One of these games consists, specifically, in this: the child, hearing two diverse explanations for the same fact, agrees to "believe" in both simultaneously. Evidently, in such instances, the truth seems to him variegated and flexible, allowing a limitless number of variations.

Here we can fully apply a very apt English word—"half belief"— meaning believing only in part, only half believing. This half believing has different levels and, at times, it seems to me that the child applies it according to his fancy.

Five-year-old Liusia once asked a motion picture director:

"Why does the tram run here and there?"

He answered: "Because the tram is alive."

"And why the sparks?"

"It is angry, wants to go to sleep, but they make him go on running —so he snorts with sparks."

"That's not true!" Liusia cried. "It isn't alive and it isn't angry."

"If it weren't alive it would not run."

"No, there is some kind of machine in it—my father told me. I know!"

The director was discouraged by her realism and fell silent. But, some time later, he overheard, to his amazement, how Liusia instructed her playmate:

"But don't you know? If it weren't alive would it run back and forth? Look!—sparks!—the trolley is angry; it wants to sleep; it is worn out with running."

Her friend listened and believed as much as was necessary to believe for the given purpose. Liusia continued to enjoy the illusion about the live and angry trolley. Although she knew perfectly well what a trolley actually was like, she obliterated this bit of knowledge from her consciousness because, for the moment, it interfered with her imaginary game. In truth, at times the child does not so much adapt himself to the truth as he adapts the truth to himself, for the sake of an imaginary play situation.

My great-granddaughter Mashen'ka, beginning at the age of two, expressed her fascination with fairy tales and their fantastic representations of the world by her use of the phrase "as if." Here is an excerpt from her mother's diary:

"She already knows perfectly well that neither animals nor objects can speak. Nevertheless, she plies me with questions:

" 'Mother, and what did the horse say to grandpa, *as if?*'

"Or:

" 'Mother, and what did the chair say, *as if*, to the table when someone moved it away? He said: "I'm lonely without the little table," *as if*, and the little table, *as if*, started crying.'

"And if I cannot always imagine what 'as if,' for example, the house said to the truck, she prompts me and asks that I repeat.

"When we go to gather mushrooms they say, *as if*, 'Let's crawl out of the ground and run, they have come for us.' "

From further entries in that same diary, it became clear that the little girl felt herself to be in full control of all the illusions she produced and could, at will, reject them when they did not suit her interests. Once, at teatime, she capriciously refused to eat her roll. Her mother attempted to influence her by means of that same "as if":

"Don't you hear?—the roll begs you to eat it."

And in answer she heard the logical reply:

"The roll can't talk. It doesn't have a mouth."

This repeated itself more than once; the child, when necessary, would immediately reject all "as if's" and would become a sober realist. She had, like all children, a purely playful attitude to fantasy and she believed in her illusions only to the extent that she needed them in her perceptive games.

The child reacts the same way to the inventions of fairy tales. A certain overwise father, seeking to protect his daughter from fantasy, composed for her an antifantasy, so to speak, in which the notion was stressed that there was no such thing as a Baba-Yaga [a traditional witchlike character in Russian fairy tales].

"I know without your telling me," the daughter replied, "that there is no Baba-Yaga; but you tell me the kind of fairy tale where there is one."

The process of arriving at the truth does not in the least strain the child. Many problems he solves instantly, extempore, on the basis of random analogies, sometimes using astonishing fantasy.

The mother was getting ready to bake some pies. The five-year-old daughter was sitting on the window sill. It was twilight. She asked:

"Where do stars come from?"

The mother was a little slow in answering—she was busy with the dough. The little girl followed her mother's motions and within a few minutes announced:

"I know how stars are made! They make them from what is left over from the moon."

This spontaneous thought was suggested to her by the process of preparing the dough for the crusts of the pies. She noticed how her mother, preparing the dough for the crust of the biggest pie, cut away from the large stretched piece the "leftover" bits and shaped from them the crusts for another dozen or so small pies.

In this way the childish mind conceived a parallel between pies and stars, which instantly led her to a new theory about the birth of the planets.[1]

This is how it is. But we must not allow these fantastic deductions to obscure from us the basic striving of the child's mind to acquire the vast amount of knowledge necessary for his proper functioning in the world.

No matter how unstable and shaky the mental life of the preschool child may seem to us (especially during the first five years of his existence), we must not forget that the child "from two to five" is the most inquisitive creature on earth and that the majority of the questions he asks are evoked by the daily need of his tireless mind to comprehend his surroundings.

"I want to ride in the sky on my bicycle, to look at the moon and the stars," says four-year-old Volodia.

And here is a stenographic transcript of the questions asked of his father, with shotgun speed, by a certain four-year-old boy, within a period of two and a half minutes:

"Where does the smoke fly?

"And bears? Do they wear a brooch?

"And who rocks the trees?

"Can one find a newspaper that is large enough for wrapping a camel?

"Is an octopus hatched from eggs or is he a mammal?

"Do chickens go out without rubbers?"

And here are the questions of another child:

"How did the sky happen?

"How did the sun happen?

"Why is the moon so much like a lamp?

"Who makes bugs?"

At times questions follow each other at a slower pace. In an unpublished diary of F. Vigdorova appear the following questions asked by her five-year-old daughter:

" 'What is a giant? Would there be enough space for a giant in our room? What if he were to stand on all fours? And by how many times is Diumovochka smaller than the giant? And how many times bigger is the giant than I? Do giants wear clothes or are they naked? And what do giants eat? Are they kind or not? Can one giant kill all the fascists?' All these questions were not asked all at once, but one by one. It means that this little brain continued to work, to ponder."

Mashen'ka asked about the radio:

"And how did all the men and women, with their music, crawl into the radio with their instruments?"

And about the telephone:

"Daddy, when I talked with you over the telephone, how did you manage to get into the receiver?"

I have been told about a three-year-old boy who posed a similar question. His aunt, a physicist by education, immediately undertook to explain to him the structure of a telephone apparatus. He listened attentively; but, after all the explanations, he asked:

"But how did daddy manage to crawl out of it?"

As the child advances in age, his knowledge-seeking efforts increasingly lose their vagueness, and already, at the age of five to six, the child begins to approach the materials for his intellectual work with great seriousness.

A young mother of the town of Pushkin wrote me very convincingly about this, in a letter about her four-year-old Nikolka:

"He stubbornly questions me about what is war, what is a country's border, what kind of people live in other countries, who fought whom and with whom did various countries live in peace, with whom our country is getting set to go to war, and what incites this country or that to go to war, and so forth. He gives me no respite; he is so insistent that it seems he wants to memorize the answers. I often refuse to answer because I do not know how to deal with a four-year-old mind; he gets annoyed and even begins to scorn me for not knowing the answers.

"How is the water pump built, the automobile, the steam boiler, the tractor, electric light, what is a storm, where do rivers come from, how does one hunt wild beasts, how do children get started in their mother's stomach—by means of food, perhaps? He wants detailed answers about birds, about marine creatures. Such are his questions; they originate completely in his mind, without any prodding from me (this maternal illusion is forgivable . . .), and they were all brought up even last year, when he was only three.

"Often I answer him good-naturedly: 'When you grow up, you'll find out, as Nekrasov has said.' In a most serious and thoughtful manner he says:

" 'If you don't answer my questions I'll remain stupid; if you don't refuse to answer them, Mommie, I'll get smarter and smarter. . . .' "

Not every child is capable of motivating his demands for information so clearly when he seeks knowledge from adults, but every child demands it with the same insistence.

This demand four-year-old Seriozha laconically expressed when he turned to his mother with these words:

"I'm a why-er, you are a because-er!" ["*Ia pochemuchka, a ty potomuchka!*"]

Adults who irritably avoid answering the "boring" childish questions commit an irrevocable and cruel act—they forcibly retard the child's mental growth and thwart his spiritual development. It is true that with some children there is a period when they literally wear out their grandmothers, fathers, and mothers with endless "Why's" and "What-for's," but what is our respect for the child worth when we deprive him, for the sake of our personal convenience, of essential mental nourishment?

The feeling of one's social responsibility for the proper education of his children prompts many mothers and fathers to occupy them-

selves strenuously with self-education—specifically in order to prepare themselves gradually for the inevitable questions of four-year-
old thinkers.

"I must confess that I often lack the knowledge for answering a
series of questions asked by my children," writes one mother in the
wall newspaper of her child's kindergarten. "The elementary information I was given in school in the fields of the natural sciences and
biology is not always adequate and is half-forgotten; at the same time
children's questions are sometimes quite varied. . . . To answer
these questions one must *know* and one must answer them in such a
way that the child understands. . . . So, one has to go to the plane-
tarium, read the book *The Truth about the Sky,* take up botany and
zoölogy." [2]

Our educational duty is not only to answer a youngster's endless
questions but also actively to stimulate his curiosity, so that, from
year to year and, at times, even from month to month, these questions may become more and more interesting.

From this, of course, it does not follow that we must all at once
crowd the child's brain with all our own heavy erudition. "To answer the questions of a child skillfully," wrote Maxim Gorki, "is a
great art; it requires caution." Our answers to children's questions
must be strictly rationed. Children do not at all demand that we dis-
close to them ultimate truths and all the truths about everything, in
all their complexity and depth. According to the observation of
Soviet educators, "even the older preschoolers do not always aim at
obtaining, by means of their questions, the full reason for this or that
phenomenon, an explanation of which can be fully given only in
scientific terms, not yet understandable to the child. Children understand mainly the peripheral and external links among various natural phenomena. For this reason the child is often satisfied with a
simple analogy or example." [3]

About the Beginning and the End of Being

We must make use of this peculiarity of the child's mind when he
poses questions which we cannot answer with complete directness.
Questions of this type include those concerning birth.

The more inquisitive children, in most instances, have already begun in their fourth year to wonder about how they appeared in the world. At that time they also begin to wonder how all that lives appeared on the earth; and there probably is not a child who does not formulate his own hypothesis on this.

Of course, all such hypotheses are, without exception, wrong; but each one of them testifies loudly to the tireless effort of the child's mind. The contemplation of the beginning of everything that exists is the law governing the mental development of the child. And when the child asks: "Who gave birth to the first mother?"—he expresses thereby one of the earliest efforts of his mind to reach out in search of the primary causes of the material world.

Experienced teachers apply a special method by means of which it is possible, without turning away too much from the truth, to satisfy the child in the early stages of his inquisitiveness, when he tries to penetrate the mystery of how human beings are born. "And why is father never pregnant?" a youngster asked his kindergarten teacher. She answered him with that "caution" recommended to teachers by Gorki: "Children are borne only by mothers but fathers also love their children and are concerned about them. You saw how the pigeons fed their baby birds—both the mother and the father gave the babies their food. Only the mother laid the eggs in the nest, but when the mother pigeon flew away for a while, the father pigeon sat in the nest and kept the eggs warm. . . ." This is the good, intelligible way to answer such questions put by children.

Whether this is the only way, I do not know. There are differences in children, and we have no universal "prescriptions." We sometimes need an individual approach; furthermore, a lot depends on the teacher's sensitivity, on his skill and tact. A general norm, equally suitable to every child under all circumstances, does not and cannot exist. For this reason we are obliged to limit ourselves in the following pages to a simple reproduction of characteristic examples illustrating how many-faceted and how ardent is the interest in these young minds in this, for them, insoluble problem.

Here, for example, is a curious note about my great-granddaughter, Mashen'ka:

"Up to the age of four she was persuaded that children were bought in stores. But, recently, after her fourth birthday, a shower of questions: 'In what kind of store? Where? How?,' and so on. We were forced to explain that children are not bought but born: the tummy is cut open and the child is lifted from it. For example, Mother gave birth to Mashen'ka, and Grandmother Marina gave birth to Mother, and so forth. 'And Grandfather Kolia—whom did he give birth to? Do women give birth to girls and men to boys?' And she was perturbed when she found out that men do not give birth and that only women's tummies are cut open. Another shower of questions: 'Why did Aunt Galia give birth to Seriozha and not you? He didn't want to be in *your* tummy? Why? And why was Liudochka born after me and now she is smaller than I? Why didn't she want to be born together with me?' "

"My six-year-old Tus'ka," writes her father, "saw a pregnant woman and said, laughing:

" 'Oh, what a belly!'

"I said to her: 'Don't laugh at the woman—there's a baby in her tummy.'

"Tus'ka, with horror:

" 'She ate up a baby?!' "

.   .   .

"Mothers give birth to boys too? Then what are fathers for?"

.   .   .

"How I was born I know. But how were you and father born?"

.   .   .

"Mother, who gave birth to me? You? I knew it! If daddy had given birth to me I'd have a mustache."

.   .   .

And, again—on the same subject:

"What kind of librarian is she? With a mustache?"

"Yes."

"And why does she have a mustache?"

"I don't know."

"Her father must have given birth to her."

.   .   .

"The rooster, could he completely, completely, completely forget that he is a rooster, and lay an egg?"

.   .   .

"What do you mean—where did I come from? You yourself gave birth to me, with your own hands."

.   .   .

"Out of what does one make people? Out of bones?"

.   .   .

"Uncle, uncle, so many tiny rabbits came pouring out of the big rabbit! Come, quicker, or they'll all crawl back and you'll never see them!"

.   .   .

"Oh, Mommie, Mommie, why did you give birth to this awful Guk? It would have been better if he had remained in your stomach forever and be lonely there all his life."

.   .   .

In Vera Panova's novel, *Seriozha,* its five-year-old hero has a discussion with himself:

"Where do children come from—that's well known: they are bought at the hospital. The hospital trades in children. One woman bought two at the same time. Why did she buy two that were alike?—they say she tells them apart by a birthmark—one has a birthmark on his neck, the other has none. It's strange; why does she need identical children? It would have been better to buy two that were different."

Generally, the legend that parents buy their children is one of the most widespread among the younger preschoolers.

A persistent, teasing old man said to five-year-old Natasha, about her younger sister:

"Give me this little girl as a gift!"

"That's impossible!" Natasha objected stolidly. "We paid money for her."

.   .   .

The father of six-year-old Svetlana had just sold his television set.

"That's good!" pronounced Svetlana. "Now you have money with which to buy me a little brother."

.   .   .

Three-year-old Irina was convinced that her mother was not "buying" a baby because babies were too expensive. With this in mind, every penny [*kopeika*] that she happened to find on the street, in the yard, or around the house she brought to her mother with the same directive:

"Only for buying the baby! Don't spend it on anything else!"

.   .   .

Ira Gmuzhina asked her mother to buy her a little Tania.

"Tanias are very expensive," the mother answered. "Would you like a doll?"

Ira refused the doll. Within a few days a decrease in prices was announced over the radio.

"Now," Ira exclaimed, "you can buy me a Tania!"

.   .   .

This happened during the war—the little girl's nanny [*niania*] had stood in line for a long time but did not receive the rations for which she came. Trying to console the disappointed nanny, the little girl said:

"Nanny, dear, don't be so upset! Mommie went to the hospital, she stood and stood in line, but instead of a boy they gave her a girl!"

.   .   .

I remember, twenty years ago, when there were still horse-drawn carriages in Leningrad, six-year-old Anton, when he found out that baby horses are born "from the belly," asked:

"But do coachmen have such a large belly?"

.   .   .

"Say, Mother, when I was born, how did you find out that I was—Yurochka?"

.   .   .

"Had I known that you'd be so mean, I'd not have gotten born to you."

.   .   .

Five-year-old Eric, boasting in the communal kitchen:

"My father promised Mother a wrist watch if she gave birth to a girl. If he'd give *me* a watch I'd bear him ten of them."

.   .   .

Not seldom do we meet children who consider various methods of procreation equally possible:

"Mommie, did you buy me or give birth to me?"

"I gave birth to you."

"Oh! But Lion'ka you bought?"

. . .

A threat:

"I'll run away to Rostov, will give birth there to a baby, and I will never write you its name."

. . .

"Why did you give birth to such a mean daddy?"

. . .

"Mommie, darling, give birth to a little one."

"Don't nag. I have no time to bear a baby."

"But you have a day off sometimes!"

. . .

"What did I see when I was in mommie's tummy?"

"You didn't see anything!"

"That's not true—when mommie opened her mouth I'd look out and see things."

. . .

"All right, if you don't want me to be your son then ungive birth to me." (Then he cried all day, oppressed by his scoffing insolence.)

. . .

"Mommie, please give birth to a baby or a puppy. I beg you! You know how much I'll love them."

I have been convinced many times over of how well the child is armored against thoughts and information that he does not yet need and that are prematurely offered to him by too-hasty adults. If the mother or the father, not taking into account the needs of the child's age, does attempt to reveal to him the full and candid truth about conception, pregnancy, birth, and so forth, he, in accordance with the laws of his childish nature, will inevitably transform this truth into material for boundless fantasy.

Five-year-old Volik Schmidt reacted in this manner when his mother openly discussed with him, at length and in detail, the process of procreating babies. He began at once to improvise a long "novel" about his life in his mother's womb:

". . . There was a partition there . . . between her back and her tummy. . . ."

"What kind of partition?"

"The kind with a door. The door was very tiny. Yes, yes—I saw it myself when I was in your insides. And there is also a tiny, tiny room there. A little uncle lived in it when I was in your tummy."

"What sort of uncle?"

"I visited him, drank tea with him. Then I played in the small garden. There was a little garden there too—with sand in it. And a little wagon. . . . I played with the kids there and took rides with them in the little wagon."

"How did the kids get there?"

"They were born to the little uncle. Many, many children. And all of them were boys—there were no girls."

"And you lived with them?"

"I often visited the little uncle, and when it was time to be born I said good-bye, shook hands with him, and came out of your belly."

This story about young Volik, who colonized his mother's womb, I borrowed from the published diary of Vera Fedorovna Schmidt. In the same diary I came across another curious entry:

"After swallowing each bite, Volik would stop and listen to what was happening inside of him. Then he would smile gaily and say:

" 'It just ran down the little ladder to the stomach.'

"What do you mean—down the little ladder?

" 'I have a little ladder there (and he pointed from the neck to the stomach); everything I eat runs down this ladder. . . . And then there are other little ladders in my arms and legs. . . . All over what I eat runs down little ladders into my body. . . .'

"Did someone tell you all this?

" 'No, I saw it myself.'

"Where?

" 'Oh, when I was in your tummy, I saw the kind of ladders you had there. . . . That means that I, too, have the same kind. . . .' "

And that is what a five-year-old child did with the embryological truths that his mother had hastened to impart to him.

The following valuable thoughts expressed by A. S. Makarenko could serve as the best commentary on the above lines from the overzealous mother's diary:

"Above all else," says this great educator, "they [parents] worry about the child's being especially well prepared for adult sex life; that he should see in sex nothing shameful, nothing clandestine. Striving for this, they try the sooner to educate the child in all the secrets of sex life, to explain to him the process of birth. Of course, they point with real 'horror' to those 'simpletons' who deceive their children and tell them fairy tales about storks and fictitious 'pro-creators.' It is assumed that, by explaining and analyzing everything about sex, the child will see nothing shameful in it and, in this way, he will surely receive the proper sex education.

". . . There is no timetable for hurrying to meet the child's 'need' to have revealed to him 'the secrets of childbirth,' utilizing for this the casual questions the child asks on the subject. Such questions do not yet express any specific curiosity about sex, nor will a postpone-ment in disclosing these facts cause any loss to the child. If the adult more or less tactfully sidetracks the child's questions and manages this with a bit of humor, a smile, the child will forget about his inquiry and will soon be absorbed in something else. But if the adult begins to discuss with him the most intimate details regarding the sex relationship between man and woman, he will inevitably encourage in the child a curiosity about sex which will, in turn, re-sult in a premature excitement of his imagination. Such knowledge, imparted to him by the adult, he does not yet need and it is useless to him, but the play of the imagination which is thus stimulated in him could be the beginning of untimely experimentation and ex-periences.

". . . We must object to the premature discussion of the sex question with children for other reasons as well. The open and un-timely discussion of sex matters leads the child to a crude and ra-tionalistic outlook on sex, which is the beginning of that cynicism with which, at times, the adult person chats lightly with others about his most intimate sexual experiences." [4]

As we have seen, the child himself turns away from the information supplied by grownups, for which he is not yet ready. He thoroughly eliminates such information from his consciousness, as if to convince the grownups that this mental food offered by them is, in this instance, not yet needed.

The mother of Tolia Bozhinskii told me:

"I explained to Tolia what pregnancy was. When Tinochka was born I talked to him at length about how she emerged from my tummy. But some time later I told him a fairy tale about a stork. After that, when anyone asked how Tinochka was born, he would say with utter conviction:

" 'The stork brought her.'

"I never told him that Tinochka was brought by a stork."

.   .   .

There were guests in the house and one of them asked about three-year-old Volia:

"Whose eyes does Volia have?"

"His father's."

"And poor daddy remained without eyes," thought Volia, and he at once formulated the following hypothesis:

"When I was not yet born, daddy had many eyes, big ones and little ones; and when mommie bought me, daddy gave me the big eyes and he left for himself the small ones."

With what delightful ease does the child solve such problems! All this is pure improvisation, akin to the inspired "impromptus" that he utters while he plays. These inspirations are as spontaneous with him as they are unexpected by his interlocutor. Not even a moment earlier does he usually know what he is going to say, but when he says it, he does so with conviction and firmness, not doubting at all the reality of his inventions.

These inventions are transitory; they are not workable hypotheses. Within a minute the child is ready to express opposite thoughts, since at times he plays games with thoughts. Even when, by accident, he happens to witness the birth of an animal, he is ready even then to explain what is going on in a most fantastic way.

V. I. Kachalov told me that when his son and his little friend,

Mitya, found out that the cat was about to give birth to kittens, they could not guess from where the kittens would make their appearance.

Mitya looked into the cat's ear and announced:

"It will be soon now! I see a little paw already."

. . .

"My mother went to a house in Moscow to buy me a brother or a sister."

"They don't sell children in the Soviet Union, only in America."

"They don't sell them in America either; they are born there from monkeys."

. . .

"Was my mother a monkey? . . . and Nadezhda Nikitichna?" (Nadezhda Nikitichna is the kindergarten teacher.)

. . .

Here is another scientific discussion about the creation of man, according to Darwin:

Nina asked her grandmother:

"Granny, were you once a monkey?"

"No, never."

"And your mother?"

"Not either."

"Then who was a monkey? Grandpa?"

"God be with you, child! No, grandpa not either."

"Oh, well, that means that my Moscow granny was the monkey."

The ones guilty for most such confusion in the minds of children are those adults who cannot wait to enrich the children with complex and complicated knowledge for which the young minds have not yet sufficiently matured. It is impossible for the young child to have any conception of the millions of years required for the evolutionary process. His idea of time is limited to the narrow scope of his minimal childish experience. Therefore, no matter how hard adults try to enlighten the child fully with scientific learning, there will always result the inevitable boomerang of confusion. When, for example, the father of six-year-old Kolia began to tell him about the evolution of the animal kingdom, the boy understood this story in his own way and informed his kindergarten friends as follows:

"I know: my grandfather used to be a monkey; he began to work and then became a man. After that he gave birth to my father, and my father gave birth to me."

For any child "from two to five," life of all humanity begins, at best, with grandfather.

Before reproducing here my notes about how small children react to the idea and the fact of death, I should like, in the form of a brief introduction, to stress one of the most splendid qualities of the child's soul—optimism. All children between the ages of two and five believe (or yearn to believe) that life is meant only for joy, for limitless happiness, and this belief is one of the most important conditions for their normal psychological growth. The gigantic task of the child in mastering the spiritual heritage of the adult world is realized only when he is satisfied with the world that surrounds him. This is the source of his incentive and strength to wage the struggle for happiness which the individual carries on even during the most trying periods of his life. I suggest you visit an osteotuberculosis hospital, where small children, bedridden for years, manage, despite their strained lives, to feel such blessed joy of living that even the pain they endure, year after year, does not traumatize them as it would adults.

A wonderful play by T. Habbe, *The City of the Masters,* was presented in a Moscow children's theater. This play was meant for older children, but my young grandson happened somehow to attend one of its performances. For a while he watched the stage with intense interest, then suddenly he shut his eyes very tightly and covered them with his palms, saying:

"I'll not look any more. Tell me when the happy part begins again."

This happened when the good and honest Hunchback Karakol', the hero of the play, fell into the hands of his enemies and the cunning villain unfairly accused him of stealing the ring that he himself had given the hunchback. The triumph of duplicity and evil over courage and honor was so unbearable to the five-year-old heart that my grandson hurried to eliminate this entire tormenting episode. He removed his hands from his eyes only when he became convinced that all the misfortunes suffered by Karakol' had passed and that he was happy once more.

Why, in general, do young children take so much to heart the fate of their beloved characters? Why do they grieve and weep when these characters are in trouble, and feel such radiant happiness when they triumph and are lucky? The main reason for this, it seems to me, is that children are capable of identifying with these characters. When my grandson closed his eyes so as not to see the suffering to which Karakol' was being subjected, most likely he did it because, identifying himself with Karakol', he felt sorry for himself. And since in children's stories the heroes are invariably fearless, self-sacrificing, honorable, and active fighters against the evil and dark forces of life, so that good may triumph, the child feels himself to be similarly a participant in this combat for the good. This is why it is so painful for him to see evil and dark forces displace goodness from the world. In such moments the child closes his eyes hard, hoping, by this noningenious method, to ensure for himself peace of soul.

"In our family," A. N. Robinson wrote me, "we treasured an old book, 'The Tales of Grandmother Tatiana.' Three generations of children, in the course of half a century (my uncles, I, and my children), knowing in advance the contents of these stories, would skip those pages (quickly turning them) where the death of the little rooster, or the way the little gray goat perished, was told."

In the famous story of "The Three Bears," a little girl loses her way in the forest and goes into the bears' cottage, breaks the little bear's chair, and eats up his soup. The bears return while she is still there and are angry with her and threaten her.

Vova disliked this story and expurgated from it all unpleasantness. In his own version, the story happened not to the little girl but to him. It was he, Vova, who lost his way in the forest and found himself in the bears' cottage. He did not break any of their furniture and, although he did eat up their soup, he immediately went to the kitchen and cooked another dish, more of it and tastier. The bears turned out to be very kind—they offered him honey and apples, presented him with a Christmas tree and gifts, and taught him how to shoot with a rifle. In a word, when the child heard the sad episodes in this story along with the jolly ones, he improvised on the original version and eliminated the parts that described the failures of the heroine, leaving in the story only what was successful and joyful.

But Alik Babenishev expressed his eagerness for an optimistic image of the world more decisively and more practically than any of the others.

"He loves books very much," his mother informed me. "He particularly liked the story about Buratino. Every day when I returned from work he would beg:

" 'Read me *The Little Golden Key*.'

"I noticed one day that a page had been torn out of the book unskillfully, showing the jagged edge of what was left of it.

" 'Who did this?' I asked.

"Alik looked away and confessed:

" 'I.'

" 'Why?'

" 'So that he would never insult her again!'

"I don't remember at the moment which of the characters insulted Malvena, but precisely that page had been torn out in which Malvena was insulted."

Generally, children intensely dislike sadness in their literature. With great resourcefulness and without anyone's help, children create for themselves illusions of happiness and watch with an eagle eye against its being ravaged.

This eagerness for the happy outcome of all human affairs manifests itself especially while children are listening to stories. When one reads to a child a story featuring a kind, fearless, noble hero fighting against evil enemies, the child invariably identifies himself with this hero. Vicariously experiencing every situation in the story, he feels himself to be a champion of truth and ardently hopes that the struggle which the noble hero is fighting will end in victory over cunning and wickedness. In this lies the great humanizing value of the story; every misfortune of the hero, even a temporary one, is lived through by the child as his own, and in this way stories condition him to take to heart other people's griefs and joys. When bandits attack the hero, when a witch transforms him into a mouse or a lizard, the child is deeply disturbed and demands, persistently, that the adversities which are the hero's lot cease as soon as possible, and that boundless happiness reign again; all this appears normal to the psyche of the child.

An eight-year-old Octobrist * once said:

"Ania, I went to see 'Chapayev' † ten times and still he was drowned at the end of the movie. Maybe if I go with my dad . . . ?"

He liked to think that the death of Chapayev had been some kind of mistake in the motion picture and that this morbid cinematic error would somehow be corrected by his father, thus ensuring that the hero, Chapayev, would not die; for this reason the tragic ending in the film about a loved hero seemed to him to be against nature and some kind of unbearable mistake. The literary characters who become dear to the child must succeed in their enterprises, and one must not, no matter what, allow them to die, since it is with them that the child identifies.

Appealing, in this connection, were the revisions that two three-year-old boys introduced into the tale of *Little Red Riding-Hood*, which someone had just told them.

One of the pair, Andreika, immediately drew an illustration for the story, in the shape of a rather misshapen mushroom, and explained to his family:

"This is a rock—the grandmother hid herself behind it. The wolf couldn't find her and didn't eat her up."

The other innovator, Nikita (nicknamed Kitya), secured for himself a similar confidence in the complete felicity of the world by expurgating from this tale all that seemed to him sad and frightening. True, this resulted in an exceptionally short fairy tale, but a completely reassuring one. Kitya told it this way:

"Once upon a time there was a little Riding-Hood and she went and opened the door. That's all. I don't know any more of it!"

"And the wolf?"

"We don't want a wolf. I'm afraid of him."

"We don't want a wolf"! The question is—could such an optimist, who would not allow any reminders of the terrors and the suffering of life, admit into his consciousness the tragic thought of death, no matter whose, to say nothing of his own?

---

* An Octobrist is a member of a nationwide Soviet children's organization, whose name derives from the October Revolution (1917).

† "Chapayev" is a Soviet motion picture whose main character was a hero of the October Revolution.

If it should come into your head to tell a young child the whole truth about death, be assured that he will, because of the perpetual childish striving for happiness, immediately take measures to replace this truth with his own myth.

Vasia Kutanian, four years old, with skepticism asked his mother:

"Mommie, do all people die?"

"Yes."

"And we?"

"We'll also die."

"That's not true. Say that you're joking."

He sobbed so intensely and pitifully that his mother, frightened, began to assure him that she had been joking. He calmed down right away.

"Of course you were joking. I knew it. At first we'll all become little oldsters [*staren'kie*] and then we'll again become youngsters [*moloden'kimi*]."

In this manner he restored his optimism, almost by [mental] force.

. . .

We recall, in this connection, Egorushka in Chekhov's story, "The Steppes":

"He imagined as dead his mother, Christopher, Countess Dranitskaia, Solomon. But no matter how hard he tried to imagine himself alone in a dark grave, far from home, forsaken, helpless, and dead, he could not; he could not admit to himself the possibility of his death, and felt that he would never die. . . ."

Optimism is as essential to the child as the air he breathes. It would seem therefore that thoughts about death would strike the severest blow against this optimism. However, as we have just seen, the child protects himself marvelously well from such sorrow. In his spiritual arsenal there are sufficient means for protecting the optimism so necessary to him. No sooner, at the end of his fourth year, is the child convinced of the inevitability of death for all living creatures, than he hastens to assure himself that he will eternally remain immortal.

A round-eyed boy, about four and a half, looked out of the bus window at a funeral procession and said, with serenity:

"Everyone will die, but I'll remain."

A craving for immortality is excellently expressed in Vera Panova's novel, *Seriozha*. [The film, "A Summer to Remember," which is one of the exchange films between the Soviet Union and the United States, is based on this novel.]

"Could it be that we'll all die?" the six-year-old Seriozha asked the grownups.

They all seemed embarrassed as if he had asked about something indecent. But he looked at them and waited for an answer.

Korostelev [his stepfather with whom he had a very good relationship] answered:

"No. We'll not die. Auntie Tosia—she can please herself about that—but we'll not die, and you, particularly, I guarantee, will not die." [Auntie Tosia was an old woman.]

"I'll never die?" Seriozha persisted.

"Never!" Korostelev promised convincingly and jubilantly.

And the boy at once felt lighthearted and wonderful. He blushed with happiness and burst out laughing. Suddenly he felt an unbearable thirst. He had felt thirsty before [the conversation], but somehow he forgot about it. Now he drank and drank, and between gulps he heaved sighs of utter delight. He had not the least doubt that what Korostelev had just told him was the truth. How would he have lived, knowing that he would die? And could he (at that age) disbelieve him who told him: "You will not die!"

.   .   .

"Mother," said four-year-old An'ka, "all the people will die. But someone will have to place somewhere the urn with the ashes of the last dead person. Let me do it! All right?"

Touching, varied, and shrewd are the many ways in which the child drives the thought of his death out of his mind. Re-creating optimism is one of the great laws of the child's life.

Totochka Harriton heard her nurse sing:

> "And no one will know
> Where is my grave."

And she began to sing it this way:

> "And no one will know
> Where is your grave."

The nurse corrected her:

"You don't sing it right. You should say 'Where's *my* grave.' "

"That's just what I did say: 'Where is *your* grave.' "

. . .

The dead seem immortal to some children.

L. M. Nikolaenko took her three-year-old Marina to the cemetery when she went there to plant a little maple tree over the grave of the child's grandmother. At home the little girl announced, after the visit to the cemetery:

"At last I saw grandmother Lida!"

"What are you talking about, Marosha! You saw only her grave."

"No, I saw her—I saw how she looked in that hole in which you planted the tree."

. . .

A five-year-old girl came to the cemetery with her mother and suddenly saw a drunkard walking unsteadily among the bushes.

"Did this uncle just dig himself out of his grave?" she asked.

. . .

Verosaev has written down the following dialogue:

"Do you know, Mother, I think that people are always the same ones: they live, and live, then they die. They are buried in the ground. After that they get born again."

"What nonsense you are talking, Glebochka. Just think—how can that be? They bury full-grown people and they are born again as babies?"

"Why not?! It's the same as with peas. The stem of the pea bush is so big—even bigger than I. Then the peas are put in the ground and they begin to grow big again."

. . .

Many years later I was told about a similar hypothesis offered by a three-year-old child:

"They bury old people—that is, they plant them in the ground and from them grow little children, like flowers."

. . .

To the very young preschooler, death may even appear as being full of pleasures. Volik was asking about a certain corpse:

"On what did he ride to his funeral?"

"Well, you saw how it's done."

"It's like taking a ride in a box. Yes?"

.   .   .

"Mommie, I want to become a military student; they play music at their funerals and their cap is placed on the coffin."

.   .   .

Uncle Shura passed away and today was his funeral.

"And will there be music?"

"No, he's not from the military."

"And you, daddy, are you military?"

"No."

"And Uncle Gaga—is he military?"

"No, why?"

"I feel like listening to music."

When children become older, the self-centered concern about their own immortality and about the immortality of their kin begins to change into the unselfish thought of the immortality of all humanity. The Ukrainian scholar, N. N. Grishko, told me about the following conversation in his family:

"Mother, will I also die?" a nine-year-old girl asked.

"Inevitably."

"Soon?"

"In about a hundred years."

The girl began to sob, saying:

"I don't want to die, mommie, I want to live a thousand years."

A pause. Then:

"Mother, do you know what? I'll study very hard and get excellent grades in everything. Then I'll study to become a doctor and will invent a medicine that will make people live forever."

"You will not succeed in doing this."

"All right. Then let people live at least a hundred years. Such a medicine I'll invent no matter what."

This conversation is delightful and remarkable because it reveals that the early childish self-centeredness is here being replaced (under our very eyes, so to speak) by a deep concern for all humanity.

.   .   .

Lialia Tsveiberg, a five-year-old, said:
"Look! All these grown-up men and women—what are they busy with—with funerals! Of course, I am not afraid. No! But it's a pity —they bury and they bury and it's human beings they bury. Let's go and inform the militia—I feel so sorry for these dead people!"

.   .   .

Literally the same emotion was expressed by another five-year-old girl, Sashen'ka:
"Why do people die? . . . I am sorry for them. I am sorry for all people, even strangers: why do they die?" (From the diary of F. Vigdorova for December 23, 1946.)

.   .   .

Five-year-old Misha had this to say when he heard about the death of a family acquaintance:
"To die—that's very bad. It's forever!"

.   .   .

Alik Babenishev thought of a good way to postpone the death of his mother:
"Mommie, now I know everything! You'll eat yogurt both in the morning and in the evening, and I'll not eat it at all. That way we'll both die at the same time."
This little boy had listened to a lecture on "Longevity" on a radio program, which stressed the beneficial role of yogurt in assuring good health and longevity.

.   .   .

The artist Konashevich writes the following about his granddaughter, Alenushka:
"She tried to persuade us and her grandmother not to die until she was grown up and would find a medicine against old age and death. 'Because there must not be any death.' "

The New Era and Children

As I have already said elsewhere in this book, I began to collect children's sayings and expressions about forty years ago, and this has given me the opportunity to notice one very important common element in the material gathered—the frequent similarity and repetition of these sayings and expressions—their running to type, so to speak. My great-granddaughter, in her word improvisations, took the same general direction that my children and grandchildren had taken; this was true not only with regard to word improvisation and creation but also in her over-all mental activity.

These three generations of children, whom I was able to observe over such a long period of time, gave, at the same age, the same cause-and-effect explanation for similar phenomena observed in the life around them. In the great majority of the letters I have received from my readers, I have found their observations similar to my own; these observations also present a similar diversity. For instance, from all ends of the Soviet Union I have been told about children who, having been informed by adults that man has descended from the ape, deduced from this that the ape was their grandfather. The same can be said about how frequently one hears the childish supposition, made by three- and four-year-olds, that girls are born only to mothers and boys only to fathers. Similarly, children from different generations invent the words "all-body's," "*smear*eline" (for vaseline), "bulleting" (for shooting), and so forth; the processes of their intellectual efforts in learning their language are the same in parts of the country distant from one another and lead to the same results (and often to the same mistakes).

However, children's thoughts and judgments reflecting their society are infinitely varied.

Four-year-old Misha Yurov was being discharged from the hospital. When his nurse was saying good-bye to him she asked:

"Misha, are you a Muscovite [*Moskvich*]?"

"No, I'm a 'Victory' [*Pobeda*]!"—the boy's answer indicated that for him, as for most boys, "Moskvich" was mainly the name of an automobile; likewise, "Pobeda."

A three-year-old boy was taking a walk in the city and saw a horse standing in the street.

"She probably doesn't have any electric current!" he said, revealing in this short phrase that a new generation of children is now with us, for whom electric trains, electric trolleys, and so forth, are better known and understood than a horse.

Not so long ago children always attributed human or animal aspects to machines:

"Mother, look at that red-cheeked bus!"

Now, however, as we notice, children are so completely surrounded by electrical technology that they associate it even with a horse.

A little girl saw an elephant in the zoo for the first time. She glanced at his trunk and said:

"This is not an elephant—this is a gas mask."

There was a time, not so long ago, when children compared gas masks to elephant trunks. Now, obviously, the reverse is true.

A two-year-old citizen whose shoelace had broken while he was running sat down on the grass to tie it, saying:

"Moto out of oder . . ."—this undoubtedly meant: "Motor out of order." Even before this child was able to pronounce the words correctly, he already knew how to apply technical terminology to his tiny shoe.

.   .   .

Kika was being given an enema. He issued commands:

"Go on, insert!"

And soon:

"Detach, detach!"

.   .   .

"Oh, Mama, what a beauty you are! Like a new motorcycle!"

.   .   .

There is a verse in my tale, *Tarakanishche:*

> Rabbits in a little trolley,
> A frog on a broomstick [*metle*].

A mother informed me that her four-year-old son, Misha, read this story in his own way:

> Rabbits in a little trolley,
> A frog in the subway [*metro*].

—the child thus modernized the means of transportation.

At about the same time I received a letter from the dramatist,

I. V. Schtok, telling me about a similar revision made by his daughter, Ika, in the same verse.

Even the color of objects is associated by today's children with machines. Someone wrote me from Leningrad about a five-year-old boy who, seeing in a book the word "summer" printed three times— in red, in blue, and in black letters, said:

"This summer—fire engine; this summer—irrigation machine; this summer—freight truck."

Soviet children now try to introduce present-day technology even into stories of long ago. A five-year-old artist, after hearing a Baba-Yaga tale, drew a hut on chicken legs and added the longest antenna to the roof!

"Surely, she listens to the radio!"

.   .   .

Iliusha Rozanov (one year and ten months old), when witnessing his first storm:

"Granny, look, what a gun salute!"

He was shown a picture of a horse harnessed to a plow:

"What is this?"

Explanation: the horse plows the field.

"Is a horse—a tractor?" he asked with great disbelief.

.   .   .

A little girl was traveling on a train with her extremely talkative mother who was having a very long chat with fellow passengers. The child, jealous and wanting some attention, finally covered her mother's mouth with her little hand, saying:

"Mother, shut off your radio!"

Here, again, is a "technical conversation," which is just the opposite of what used to be observed in children's speech thirty years ago. At that time the radio would have been associated with a human mouth —and not the reverse.

Anything that was not connected with technology was uninteresting and even a deadly bore to four-year-old Anton Ivanov. Whatever else anyone would read to him he would listen to absent-mindedly and unwillingly, or hardly at all. But, as soon as he was being told about radio speakers, dynamos, and even about the ordinary electric bulb, his little round cheeks would get flushed, and running all around the room in great excitement, he would ply the storyteller with a hundred questions and would not desist until he got an answer to all his "How's," "Why's," and "What-for's."

His speech was oversaturated with technical terms. For instance, not long ago, he said (I am citing this with stenographic exactness):

"I am as exhausted as a 120-volt electric bulb connected with a 22-volt circuit—without a transformer."

All this seemed to me so incredible because the boy's family was very remote from things technical; his grandfather was a writer (Vsevolod Ivanov), his grandmother was a translator of novels and short stories, his mother—a linguist, his father—an artist, one uncle —a philologist, another—a landscape painter.

.   .   .

"This church is closed."
"Are they taking inventory?"

.   .   .

We spoke earlier in the book about a child who called a half-moon "a broken moon." Recently I was told about a boy (three and a half years old) who, during the war, cried out once:

"Mother, Mother, the moon was bombed!"
This was his reaction to the half-moon.

.   .   .

"The stars in the sky are not real ones—they are not red, not like the ones we see on holidays."

.   .   .

"When it is day here, it is night in America."
"Serves them right, those capitalists!"

.   .   .

The daughter of a wardrobe man said, when she heard that he was too ill to go to work that evening:

"What about the Five-Year Plan?"

.   .   .

Six-year-old Igor—to his mother:
"You are my most beautiful, my best, my peace-loving one."

One boy (a preschooler) was listening with fascination to a story by Pushkin about Czar Saltan. But as he listened he seemed to become preoccupied, worried, and puzzled. He wanted to know who this Czar Saltan was—on the one hand he seemed a sympathetic character; on the other, he was too much under the influence of the Witch and her cunning friends. The child kept interrupting the storyteller with questions about this incomprehensible czar:

"Was he all right? Was he a good man? Was he like one of our own —like a Soviet man?"

I read about this child in a recent article by Professor A. V. Zaporozhets.[5]

A similar reaction on the part of a ten-year-old child was recorded in the unpublished diary of F. Vigdorova. She was doing a crossword puzzle with her daughter, Galia, and they had to fill in a space with the name of a "celebrated Soviet poet." Galia suggested:

"Nekrasov." *

"In what sense is he a Soviet poet?" the mother disagreed.

"How can he not be a Soviet poet? He is such a good man!"

As they are for Galia, "Soviet" and "good" are synonymous for millions of our young citizens, including the preschool children.

Since these patriotic feelings are so well developed in both the younger and the older children, I consider it justifiable to overlook, for the moment, the child within the age range to which this book is devoted and to cite another entry in F. Vigdorova's diary—this time quoting her seven-year-old Sasha. (This entry was written on December 23, 1949.)

"If I had a magic wand, I would first of all make Vladimir Ilyich [Lenin] come to life again. Then I would revive Galia's father. Then I'd bring back to life all the great and good people from the entire past. Then I would use the magic wand just once more to bring communism everywhere."

.   .   .

Tania was eating, for the first time, some Chinese nuts.

---

* Nikolai Nekrasov (1821–1877), the renowned Russian poet whose verses championed the abused serfs and whose poetry became widely known and was recited throughout the land. He is one of the most adored poets in the Soviet Union.

"Chinese people are very kind," she said. "They put into every nut, for us, two seeds, and in some even three."

*   *   *

"What kind of a dog is this?"
"A German shepherd."
"Did he surrender? Yes?"

The basic standards and values of Soviet life have become part of the consciousness of the entire population. Children are saturated with them "up to their necks." From time to time one hears a youngster champion a standard vis-à-vis a grownup. The father of Svetik Gusev was teasing his wife:
"I give the orders around here and you must obey me."
Svetik flew at his father like a vulture:
"We no longer have such husbands these days! No one needs such a husband! You are a *past* one!"
Obviously, he meant to say "from former times."

*   *   *

"Is your father a communist?"
"No! What sort of a communist would *he* make? He quarrels with Mother every day."

In general, the great majority of young children develop their own kind of immunity to clericalism. The writer, Rudolph Bershadsky, told me the following:
"In the presence of my four-year-old daughter, I once said that my nurse used to take me to church with her all the time. My daughter interrupted my story with skepticism, saying:
" 'Daddy, is it possible that you were born so long ago—when there was still a God?' "

The childish reaction we are about to describe expresses to what extent the new feeling of social ownership has penetrated into the consciousness of the Soviet youngster:
Svetik saw an elephant at the zoo for the first time. He examined the huge beast closely and finally asked:
"And whose elephant is he?"

"He belongs to the State."

"That means that he is a little bit mine, too," Svetik concluded with great satisfaction.

The enjoyment of common ownership (with the State) I noticed first and primarily among older children. Now we begin to observe it in the preschool child as well.

In literature this feeling has been vividly expressed by the poet V. V. Mayakovsky: "The street is mine, the houses are mine"; "Mine are the deputies"; "In my Moscow Soviet"; "My militia protects me . . ." (from the poem "Good!").

One of the remarkable things about our present era, as it affects our young children, is the extraordinary amount of interest our citizens, from all walks of life, have shown in them. Quite typical is the letter I received from an engineer—a total stranger to me:

"Esteemed Comrade Chukovsky! We turn to you, as a children's author, for advice of a rather unusual nature. In connection with the awaited birth of our child, my wife and I would like to keep a 'chronicle' of his life from o to 3–4 years of age, so as to create a [written] 'photograph' of the development of our offspring—his feelings, speech, and physical growth. . . ."

This child had not yet been born, but his parents already felt a deep regard for him and his "future" feelings, speech, and actions; they believed so intensely in the importance of his psychological development, even before he appeared in the world, that they got ready to become his "chroniclers," ascribing great importance to this task for which they asked the advice of a professional writer.

Even more characteristic, in this regard, is a letter received by the children's poet, Agnia L'vovna Barto, from a pair of young parents:

"At what age should one offer Pushkin to children? When should they read Mayakovsky?"

At the time they wrote to poet Barto their child was four months old.

With what indifference early childhood was regarded in the past may be surmised from the brief and shallow sentences in the *Notes of Actor Shchepkin:*

"My childhood started and ended and was quite as uninteresting (?!) as the early years of every (?!) child."

To illustrate more graphically the vast difference between the old and the new attitudes to the child, I offer here two letters which were received in the distant past:

The first was written almost fifty years ago by an incensed *barynia* [a woman from the upper class], who had read in a newspaper my first observations on the speech of small children:

"As far as children's speech is concerned," she wrote, "I'd advise you to read the Bible; you'll find out there how three thousand years ago the wise Solomon proved that children don't know how to speak. And I, a mother of many children, can prove to you that children, because of their lack of development of feelings and brain, can only jabber and distort the words they hear spoken by adults, etc."

This letter had a postscript:

"You forget that the eggs do not teach the chicken."

In this last line was expressed a thousand-year-old lack of appreciation of the young child, which only our epoch could eradicate.

The second letter, addressed to my publisher, accompanied the first one:

"Your readers, of course, could not possibly regard Chukovsky's article, 'About Children's Speech,' as anything but a Christmas-time jest. But there should be a limit to all jokes. . . . The demise of your newspaper will occur soon if you don't stop having as your collaborators 'people from the eleventh *verst* [measure of distance].' "

She was referring to the insane asylum.

To make a study of children's early speech was then considered insane. To reveal one's esteem of the child meant, at that time, to inflict upon oneself the "public's" contempt.

Now, here is a letter I received in the thirties, from a rural scholar:

"Comrade Chukovsky! I have decided to start a diary and to enter in it expressions of little people, our future builders of socialism. I beg you to inform me how best to approach this task. I await, impatiently, your advice. Regards. Stepan Rodianov."

This letter was somewhat dry—a business letter. However, Stepan Rodianov never doubted that the way children acquire their native language has a cultural importance. For him this matter was clear— a respect for the psychological and mental experiences of the child had become part of his "flesh and blood," together with other aspects of Soviet culture. He merely wanted to know about the best methods for this difficult work, which he voluntarily assigned to himself, seemingly without sentimental posturing but simply as a civic duty. And he did not lack civic obligations! In his next letter he wrote:

"The local Soviet appointed me as cultural leader. I now have to make sure that before I can be reëlected to the Soviet, I liquidate all illiteracy and semi-illiteracy among the adults in my district."

He was a born educator. His concern with children, his concern about their orientation to their linguistic heritage, was for him a natural feeling.

In former times we literary people received correspondence mainly from mothers and grandmothers. Now letters reach us on the subject of children from young unmarried women, bachelors, and adolescents—that is, from people formerly indifferent to children. Now love of the child is not limited to mother love but is felt in millions of hearts throughout the land.

Here is a letter that is typical of the kind I now receive by the dozen:

"I am a student in a Leningrad high-technical school [VTUZ]; I am not an educator, nor a father of a family, and, as a result, I am far removed from the world of children, but . . ."

And here is a typical expression (restrained and even timid) of an overwhelming attraction to the "world of children":

"In six weeks I'll graduate from the Saratov ten-year school," writes student Natasha Nikoliukina. "I never had any brothers or sisters, but . . ." A similar confession follows.

And here is a letter from a Moscow student:

"I am awfully fond of children—clever ones and stupid ones, pretty ones and ugly ones, and I react with tenderness and rapture to all their words and acts. I'd like to know them better and understand them better. How to love them better I don't need to learn. . . . I'd very much like to become a good pediatrician who knows how to treat his little patients gently, sensitively, and attentively."

This new feeling about children has been expressed with great depth and power in Soviet literary works. The young child has become an adored hero of such writers as Arkadi Gaidar, Boris Gitkov, Vera Panova, L. Pantileev, L. Voronkova, and others.

Outstanding in its significance, and reflecting the new status of the child in our new era, is the novel by Vera Panova, *Seriozha*, published last year [1958]. What writer of the past—great or inferior—would have decided to devote an entire novel—not a story, or a sketch, but a real novel, to the representation of the feelings and thoughts of a most ordinary little boy and, in addition, make him the central character of the book? This has never happened before in our literature. This happened only as a result of the widespread interest in the young child expressed in recent years by a variety of people in every part of our land.

CHAPTER III

Children and Their Poetry

HOW CHILDREN MAKE UP VERSE

Rhythm

Among the various methods used by children in their efforts to learn their spoken language, the arrangement of words in certain patterns plays a significant role. The child thinks of words in pairs; he assumes that every word has a "twin"—an opposite in meaning or quality. Having learned a word, he already begins, toward the age of three, to look for another that is related to it. Of course, in the process of discovering these other words he makes many mistakes:

"Yesterday it was raw outside," someone remarked.

"And today—is it cooked?" a child wanted to know.

Or:

"This is running water."

"Is there sitting water?"

In such instances the children have not found the right antonym, but their attempt at classifying the words is nevertheless fruitful and has made the meaning of both clearer.

These word pairs, so far as I could observe, appear to the child to be matched not only in meaning and description but also in sound:

"Yesterday you were curly and today you are stringly," a little boy said to a neighbor who had just washed all the curl out of her naturally stringy hair.

At times the particular way in which children pair off words constitutes their attempt at rhyming:

> running—sitting
> curly—stringly

Adults, too, have a tendency to use words in rhymed pairs, but the tendency is much stronger in young children. When such rhyming occurs spontaneously in conversation, the child plays around with the verse, repeating it several times, and sometimes uses it as an improvised song:

"Where did you put the broom?" the mother asked the boy.

"Over there, on the stair," he pointed.

And no sooner did he utter the words than he noticed that there was rhythm and rhyme in them, and he began to chant:

> "Over there—
> On the stair.
>
> "Over there—
> On the stair."

Almost all children delight in games based on rhythmic rhymes, and they respond to them not merely with pleasure but even with rapture. Three-year-old Galia invented this game:

"Mother, say 'clumsy.' "

"Clumsy."

Galia rhymes: "Mumsie."

"Mother, say 'Llama.' "

"Llama."

Galia giggles and rhymes: "Mama."
"Mother, say 'salami.' "
"Salami."
Galia roars with laughter: "Mommie."
And the game goes on and on. At times a similar game-exercise in rhyming goes on for ten or more minutes.

In a kindergarten near Moscow, a group of older children often played the following game which would be started spontaneously. One of the children would say, "Let's play rhyming," and the group would take turns in finding suitable words: "boys—toys," "good—food," "pretty—kitty," and so on. Or they would merely combine a word with some senseless rhyming syllables: "trunk—munk—lunk," and the more senseless the multiple word the louder and more giddy the laughter.

I have also heard children make up rhymed monologues. Five-year-old Vova was the author of the following soliloquy:

> Is this a spoon?
> No—it's a balloon.
>
> Is this a fork?
> No—it's a stork.
>
> Is this a stove?
> No—it's a "Vov."

And so on—for a long time. And this is what three-and-a-half-year-old Tania did with the word milk:

> Ilk, silk, tilk
> I eat kasha with milk.
>
> Ilks, silks, tilks
> I eat kashas with milks.

Children who have just begun to talk in phrases make use of rhyme to ease the task of pronouncing two words in a row. It is easier for the very young child to say "night-night" than "good night," "bye-bye" than "good-bye." It seems that the younger the child the greater is his attraction to word repetition that rhymes. This may sound like

a paradox but it is confirmed by the facts. In the numerous parents'
diaries that I have read, I have often come across descriptions of the
"speech" habits of their one-year- or one-and-a-half-year-old children.
There would be observations such as the following: "Endlessly he
jabbers rhymed nonsense—for hours he 'talks' to himself in rhymed
syllables: alia, valia, dalia, malia."

It would be difficult to find more useful phonetic exercises than
these rhymed syllables, in their great variety. The rhyming is merely
the by-product of the tireless effort the child performs with his
speech organs—a very useful by-product because he experiences this
effort as play. Even before the age of one, when the child still spends
most of the day in his crib, when he cannot yet say a single word, he
already amuses himself with rhythmic jabbering, repeating again and
again some favorite sound.

In the beginning of our childhood we are all "versifiers"—it is
only later that we begin to learn to speak in prose. The very nature of
an infant's jabbering predisposes him to versifying. The word
"mama" with its symmetrical syllabic repetition is a kind of model
for rhyming. Quite a number of a child's first words have the same
pattern: daddy, nanny, granny, baby, mommie. Of course these words
and their combinations do not constitute verse. Making up verses
begins when the aimless pronouncing of rhymed and other sounds
stops and meaning is introduced.

First Poems

There is hardly a child who does not go through a stage in his preschool years when he is not an avid creator of word rhythms and
rhymes. I became aware of this many, many years ago when I observed my four-year-old son running around our garden, mounted on
a broomstick, shouting, like one possessed, a poem he had just composed:

> I'm a big, big rider,
> You're smaller than a spider.

He composed these lines for his sister's benefit, and, although she
soon ran away from the lyric taunt, he continued his frantic ride
seeing nothing, hearing nothing, and repeating, like a sorcerer's refrain:

> I'm a big, big rider,
> You're smaller than a spider.

He went around in large circles, deafened by his own cries. Suddenly, as if coming from a thousand miles away, he heard:
"Dinner!"
He was led to the washstand, then placed at the table. But his poet's blood had not yet calmed down, for the excitement of his recent rhythmic galloping had not yet subsided. Scanning with his spoon, he declaimed:

> Give me, give me, before I die,
> Lots and lots of potato pie!

The spoon helped his inspiration because the child needs to be in motion either with his hands or his feet when he composes his jingles. Another day, attaching a rag to his belt, the same boy ran from room to room, clapping his hands and singing at the top of his voice:

> I'm a whale,
> This is my tail.

Children usually think up rhymes as they hop or jump. When they make soap bubbles and see them soar, it is natural for them to jump after them, crying out not once but many times:

> How high, ai, ai, ai,
> Up to the sky, ai, ai, ai.

When children get tired and stop their running, jumping, and skipping, their composing of rhymes also comes to an end. The sad, sickly, or sleepy child will not produce a single line of verse. To become a poet the youngster must be full of animal spirits. In the early spring, on the fresh green grass, when children become pixilated from the wind and the sun, they could go on and on pouring forth verse to express their exhilaration. Often these rhymes grow out of ecstatic, rhythmic movement, are meaningless, and fulfill mainly the function of accompanying music. This inclination of small children to get "drunk" on melodic rhymes accounts for the nature of many nursery songs in Russian, Serbian, Czech, Swedish, Finnish, and English folklores.

In order not to clog up this book with too many polyglot examples, I shall limit myself to English folklore, where one finds, for example, rhymes very popular among children, such as:

> Heetum, peetum, penny, pie,
> Pop a lorie, jinkie jie!

> Eena, meena, mina, mo,
> Bassa, leva, lina, lo!

These lines mean nothing, but they are dear to English children because of their rhythm and melody, just as Russian children, from generation to generation, respond to nursery rhymes such as this one:

> Ten', ten', poteten' . . .
> Postriguli, pomiguli . . .
> Kolia, molia, selenga . . .
> Peria, eria, sukha, riukha . . .
> Tsyken', vyken' . . .

How children love the music of rhythm and rhyme! Little Mura, only four, was playing a game in which she was a hare who had many baby hares. She was so taken with her game that she soon began to talk in rhyme. I was not listening too closely but my attention was intrigued by the following amazing lines:

> The little rabbit was fast and lean
> He was chased by a Magazine.

"Magazine?" I asked. "Why, Magazine?"
She had been caught unawares, blushed, but regained her poise in a moment and explained:
"Don't you understand? Magazine—is a certain kind of rabbit. . . . He reads magazines, magazines, magazines—so they called him Magazine." Thus she gave, as an afterthought, the "logical" motivation for the rhyme which originally had no relation to the subject matter of her play. Children often distort words to achieve rhyming. Little Natochka, two and a half, made up these lines:

> The duckling and the big goose
> Sit on the broken sail-oose,

instead of "sail." Three-year-old Lena was drawing with her crayons and repeating rhythmically:

> The red house
> Made of strouss,

instead of "straws."

Young children adore nonsense rhymes. And such rhymes are very infectious. It is enough for one child to utter a rhymed series of sounds for the rest of a group to react to it with clapping, jumping, hopping, and galloping while they repeat the sounds over and over again. At times they are moved to compose rhymes by the rhythm of the motions involved in some task they are performing. I witnessed the birth of such a poetic composition one summer, in the country, when I daily accompanied a group of small children when they went to fetch a pail of water from a neighbor's well. The children carried the small pailful suspended from a stick which they held up at each end. The path on which they walked back with the water was narrow and uneven—there were rocks and roots and stumps to stumble over. After each sixteen paces their arms would get tired and the tiny water carriers had to lower the pail and take a short rest. Pretty soon, as the children became aware of the rhythm of this procedure, they made up this work chant:

> Two stumps
> Two roots
> On the road
> On the path—
>
> Don't spill it!
> Don't drop it!
> DOWN!

Sixteen feet up to "down." They would stop, rest, then walk on again, taking sixteen steps! At the word "down," shouted very loudly, the entire crew would fall down as if shot.

Then, of course, there are children's taunts which we also find in all folklore:

> Gypsy ipsy
> You're tipsy.

> Nicky bicky,
> He's tricky.

Children make up rhyming taunts not only about people but also about animals that they dislike. Once, in a village I was visiting, I noticed daily a group of children passing by a mill whose owner kept a turkey. For some reason they accused this turkey of stealing a piglet, and they chanted as they walked by the mill:

> Turkey, turk, red, red nose,
> He stole our little pigly.
> They caught him by his big toes—
> My, but he was wiggly.

These lines were voiced with great hostility. But, to be fair, I must add that within only a few days I met the same group marching in a festive mood, carrying a board laden with colorful flowers, fruit, and mushrooms—they were walking in the direction of the same mill.

"Where are you going?"

"To the turkey. Today is his birthday."

They were going to celebrate the turkey's birthday, bringing him beautiful gifts, having completely forgotten their contempt for the "thief" which they had expressed so recently in their "deathless" poetry.

Another quality of children's rhymes and nonsense verse is that they are saturated with joy. They do not show a trace of tears or a whisper of a sigh. They express the child's feeling of happiness with himself and his world which every healthy child experiences so much of the time. This is the reason that their rhymes and nonsense verse have such a zestful spontaneity.

I doubt that Friedrich Schiller was as happy when he wrote his "Hymn to Joy" as was three-year-old Bubus, crying out blissfully:

> Grandma thinks I'm dandy,
> She always brings me candy!

This was a hymn to self-assertion and bragging. To assert himself and to boast is natural for every young child, since he needs the illusion that he is more loved, more skillful, more clever, stronger, braver than others. No one is so self-satisfied as a two-year-old; it gives him endless delight to amaze himself constantly with his imaginary successes and talents. With what arrogance did the young boy, already mentioned, utter the word "I" when he teased his little sister as he sped along astride a broomstick:

> I'm a big, big rider,
> You're smaller than a spider.

I remember returning home one day and being met outside by my two youngsters who, clapping and hopping, chanted:

> We had a burglar!
> We had a burglar!

This, to them, was something unusual but excitingly gay, and they could not understand why I did not share their feeling about the matter. And here is a little boy's verse spontaneously composed and inspired by the unexpected arrival of his daddy from a journey:

> Daddy came on the train;
> The locomotive was great,
> He brought daddy early and not late.

However, within another year or two, subdued, minor notes appear in children's poems. Five-year-old Mura, looking over her birthday gifts at her birthday party, said in elegiac tones:

> If each Sunday
> Were my birthday—
> It would be great!

And she sighed at the inevitability that such an ideal must remain merely a wish. By the time children are six or seven years old, they progress from emotionally exclamatory verses to a more literary genre. Six-year-old Ania composed the following lines about her mother, after she witnessed a spanking given another child by his angry aunt:

> My mama is clever
> She spanks me never.
> Hey, mommie, mommie,

> Always love, love me—
> I now love you double,
> And will give you no trouble.

As the child grows older he is more likely to compose free verse, since clapping and chanting are now displaced by thought and introspection. For instance:

> I saw an apple
> In the royal garden—
> I did not envy it:
> It was behind bars—
> Behind bars.

This "elegy," written by a nine-year-old boy is, in reality, a comment on slavery. To have insisted here on a rigid structure and rhyming would only have spoiled this fine poem. A similar absence of regular rhythm is noticeable in the following (also excellent) "elegy" written by an older child:

> Among the gloomy rocks
> A solitary fir tree grows
> At the edge of the sea.
> Its moans go out to the sea:
>
> "Waves, dear ones!
> You pour your bitter salt water
> Over my tender skin and
> You cause me pain, great pain!
> Waves, dear ones, be merciful!"
>
> But the sea hears not the moans of the tree.

There is an in-between age, when the child is no longer at the age of "from two to five" and no longer indulges in spontaneous versifying with the stimulus of clapping and stamping or jumping; nor is he now old enough to be able to compose free or more structured verse that would satisfy him. During this period, when the child does not have the ability to satisfy, with his own creations, his hunger for the harmony and melody of poetry, he satisfies it with other poets' poetry; and at times he experiences the lyrical feeling in these poems so intensely that, in his innocence, he is inclined to regard himself as the author of this or that moving verse:

"Grandmother," said eight-year-old Vera, "write down in my note-book these lines:

"The silent sea, the azure sea!"

"But these are not your lines; Zhukovsky * wrote them."

"Yes. But they are mine too. . . . Let them be mine *and* his—ours!"

"Where did you learn them?"

"I'm telling you, I didn't *learn* them—I made them up myself. They are about the Crimea—don't you understand?"

I was informed by a mother of a similar occurrence:

"One morning Svetik woke up with a preoccupied air and de-manded that I dress him quickly.

" 'I want to write down a poem; this time it is not for children but for grownups.'

"Svetik sat down at the table, took up his pencil, and sat there for a while, thinking. Soon he said:

" 'You know what, Mother? I'll write "Alone I walk out onto the road" [*Vykhozhy odin ya na dorogu*].'

" 'But this is not your poem, it is Lermontov's.' †

" 'But Lermontov is dead, mommie, let it be mine now.' "

Only a person who does not in the least understand children would call this child, or little Vera, a plagiarist. Children's attempts to appropriate famous lines of beautiful poetry are rare. Most often they try to satisfy their love of poetry by imitating their favorite poets.

The products of this imitation are more often than not chaos rather than poetry. Reading such verse I sigh with longing for the rhythmic and colorful nonsense rhymes of children "from two to five."

Education for Poetry

Just the same, we must not be severe in judging the poetry of older children. No matter how bad and dreary their verses are and how

* Vassily Zhukovsky (1783–1852), a poet and humanitarian, was the tutor of the young Prince Alexander who later became Czar Alexander II who freed the Russian serfs.

† Mikhail Lermontov (1814–1841) was one of the great Russian poets.

far removed from movement and song, they are still a higher stage of
the child's poetic development, precisely because they no longer depend on clapping and chanting. Up to the age of about four the child
was poet, singer, and dancer—all at the same time—but now poetry
has become, for the first time, a creative activity separated from any
other art, and therefore represents a more advanced cultural endeavor.

Children begin to understand and to use metrically correct
rhythms in their poetry at about the age of ten. Here is a satirical
iambic couplet (almost perfect) of a nine-year-old girl from a pre-
revolutionary generation, about a tyrannical teacher:

> There sits our tormentor—
> The pencil tapper.
>
> [*Sidit muchitel'nyi,*
> *Karanndashom stuchitel'nyi*]

And another girl wrote this lament:

> The exam
> Like a stone
> Fell on her heart,
> And long,
> Too long,
> Hurt deep like a dart.
> She waited, my Nina, for time to pass,
> To pass the exam, and to lift the stone.

Although many of the poems written by school children are imi-
tative, some of these children could develop into good poets if they
were given adequate guidance by their teachers. Of course no one
expects teachers to train poets, but they should consider it as one
of their tasks to develop in their students an appreciation of good
poetry. This matter is very close to my heart because I belong to
that society of odd people who love poetry more than any other art,
and who know from experience the incomparable joys that poetry
affords those who know how to delight in it.

But what do our teachers do to advance the education of our children in poetry?

No matter where I find myself, without wasting any time, I go straight from the boat or the train to the children of the town or the village—to the kindergarten or the child center, or the school. In all these I am invariably cheered by the concern and the tender care for the children which I observe. But in this barrel of honey there is a spoonful of tar. When the children sing, clap, play, or work out a project, I look on with the greatest pleasure. When they begin to read me poems that have been taught to them in school or in boarding school, I often feel like a real martyr.

Together with the works of our classical poets, they have been taught hackneyed lines, absurd rhythms, cheap rhymes. There are times when I could cry with disappointment. I am convinced that exposing children to such trash will cripple their aesthetic tastes, disfigure their literary training, and condition them to a slovenly attitude to the written word, and that all this rubbish will block off the children's appreciation of genuine poetic works. However, my author's grief was incomprehensible to some of the educators, as these excellent people (so useful in other ways) had been deprived of literary culture. They had no criteria for evaluating works of poetry.

In almost every kindergarten and every child center, in every school, I met promising children, who, under different circumstances, could be developed into good writers; but their giftedness withered in the nonliterary environment in which they found themselves. The "corrections" made in their verses by the teachers were almost invariably worse than the original version.

Fortunately, this incompetence in dealing with children and their poetic education is gradually becoming a thing of the past. Thanks to the vanguard of educators such as E. A. Flerina and E. I. Tikheiva, and to their students and disciples, education for poetry is beginning to be part of the basic curriculum of the kindergarten. With love and deep thought was written the famous book published by the Academy of Pedagogic Sciences, *The Language Arts and the Preschool Child* (1952). The editor of this book, E. A. Flerina, speaks very well in her introduction both about the "musical painting" of poetry and the "melodic illustration" of poetic imagery, and about the methods of developing "feeling for rhythm" in the young child.

Another book on this theme, *Reading Books to the Kindergarten*

Child, has recently been published; its author is R. I. Zhukovskaya. The book came out in 1955. It is devoted almost entirely to the study of the educational value of poetry to the preschool child. Evidently the author became convinced, through experience, that the most nourishing and wholesome spiritual food for the kindergarten child is indeed poetry and not prose. The basic idea of this book is expressed in the words of V. G. Belinsky * regarding the effect of poetry on the very young—words that Zhukovskaya quotes on one of the first pages of her book: "Let their ear be attuned to the harmony in the Russian language, in the Russian heart, to fill them with feeling for the exquisite; let poetry also react on them as music— through the heart. . . ." [1] I read this book with the deepest pleasure. Not so long ago all discussion of the education of children in poetry struck most educators as a harmful and meaningless heresy—and now from their midst come forth people who defend this "harmful heresy" through practice.

Now I should like to speak about my own experience in training children. As I educated my own children, I tried to instill in them, from an early age, a sense of literary discrimination, of aesthetic sensibility, and thus to arm them forever against every variety of literary banality. The material that seemed to me best for reaching this goal was, of course, folklore—and, primarily, the heroic epic. I read epic poetry to my children and their numerous friends. I became convinced how nonsensical and unfounded are the fears of those adults who think that children will not understand this kind of poetry. One need only get them used to the unfamiliar locutions and they will be ready to listen for hours to these works of genius in which there is so much childlike enchantment. The very vocabulary of most epic poems, although it seems at first strange and somewhat frightening, will soon become accepted by the children as lively, clear, and exciting; and they will not only learn to love it and understand it, but they will soon begin to introduce it into their daily speech, thus helping to enrich it.

The results of this early contact with heroic poetry appeared in the writing of my young son, Boris. To the utter amazement of the

---

* Vissarion Belinsky (1811–1848) was the brilliant founder of Russian literary criticism.

adults around him, he had hardly begun to learn to spell when he started to compose a cycle of epic poems which he wrote down in his notebook—a "manuscript" that I shall always treasure. I will cite here one of them just as he wrote it, except for corrections in spelling. The date was 1919; someone carelessly told, in the presence of the child, about a rumor that had been spread all over our town that a band of night bandits could jump higher than the houses by means of particularly resilient springs installed in their boots. These bandits were said to come out at night, dressed in shrouds, to panic and burglarize the populace. The city guard was carrying on a constant battle with them.

My eight-year-old son "immortalized" these "springers" in the following [beginning lines of a sixty-eight–line] "epic" poem:

THE BATTLE OF THE SPRINGERS AND VAS'KA THE BOOTMAKER

Gold does not melt with gold,
Silver does not blend with silver,
Nor do two mountains merge into one—
But from all over the Springers gather,
They meet in the graveyard of Smolensk—
In the Smolensk graveyard so vast.
And they think vast thoughts—
Vast thoughts, not small:
How to vanquish the guard of Petrograd—
The guard of the city of Peter.

It is clear that this young poet had full knowledge of the difficult genre of the epic—its rhythm, syntax, locutions—and that he used it with ease. When Boris grew up he did not make literature his specialty, but his love for this immortal poetry enriched his life to the end of his days. This love also gave him the discriminating taste that enabled him to find his way in the labyrinths of literary works, distinguishing genuine art from every kind of literary sham.

More about First Attempts at Composing Verse

We must return now to the child "from two to five." We know that nonsense verses are:

1. Spontaneous and inspired by merriment.
2. That they are not so much songs as melodic exclamations.
3. That they are not recited but spoken with an accompaniment of clapping and "dancing."
4. That their rhythm is a trochee.
5. That they are brief—not more than two lines in length.
6. That they are repetitive.
7. That they are "infectious" among children.

But this does not mean that preschool children compose only nonsense verse. These very young children are capable of composing verse with meaning. To what extent they can do this, it is too soon to tell, since we have very limited collections of this kind of poetry. It is thus too early to draw conclusions and make generalizations. I have only a few such poems to present here; a correct evaluation of these few poems can be made only after we gather about five·or six thousand samples and classify them according to the surroundings in which they were conceived.

Here is a ballad by a four-year-old boy, Nikita Tolstoy:

> The raven looked at the moon-oon-oon
> And saw in the sky a yellow balloon
> With eyes, nose, and mouth in a round face,
> Swimming with clouds at a slow pace.

As befits every traditional ballad, we have here a raven, night, the moon. The poem is solid; its rhythm is clear,. and the rhyming is fairly precise. Another ballad, by the same author, is about seafaring:

> A pretty boat
> Sails on the sea,
> Sails on the sea.
>
> A herring is afloat
> Behind the boat—
> In the sea,
> In the sea.

And Nikita's three-and-a-half-year-old brother, Mitia Tolstoy, made up this song about the city:

Eh, fellows, duck, duck, duck,
Or you'll get run over by a truck.

Eh, fellows, run fast and far,
Or you'll get run over by a car.

Eh, fellows, let out a howl,
Or you'll get run over by a fowl.

Even on the basis of these few short poems, we can see what a variety of metric forms are used by young children. Of course Nikita and Mitia are not typical children; their parents are both writers (A. N. Tolstoy and Natalia Krandievskaia). But here are some lines by Irina Ivanova, the three-and-a-half-year-old daughter of a factory physician:

THE STUPID CAT

The cat sees a pit
And swallows it.
Off to the hospital with her.

THE WOLF AND THE HEN

The wolf walks along the street,
Sees three little hens—a treat!
To catch them he must jump the fence:
"Get ready, get set, go!"
Hens! Beware! Here comes your foe!

In most of these children's poems the rhyming is close together—children do not like the rhyming to be intermittent. This should indicate to children's writers that they must not separate rhyming lines with three or more that do not rhyme. One cannot find in folk tales a single poem—neither in Pushkin nor in Ershov,* for instance—in which the rhyming is not in consecutive lines.

We should place in a special category the verses that are monologues of lonely children, verses composed while the children are absorbed in some long, dramatic play. Such was the poem of a five-year-old bedridden child who was playing "war" as he composed it. In its twenty-two lines there were only two adjectives; the adverb

---

* Pyotr Ershov (1815–1869), a Russian poet, was the author of the famous fairy tale in verse, *The Little Humpbacked-Horse* (*Konek-Gorbunok*).

"fast" appeared eleven times; verbs were used eighteen times—there was not a single line without a verb. Verbs and not adjectives predominated—action and movement. This is characteristic of most poems of preschool children. And here is the monologue of our poet-patient:

> Soldiers speed, speed to war,
> They speed to meet the Red Army.
> They shoot fast.
> Fast fly the bullets
> And fast they meet other bullets;
> Fast they go straight into the enemy.
> Straight to war—one, two, three!
> Understand, now faster, now faster.
> Battle—boom-boom-boom . . .
> Stop! Here! The Army!
> Guns in position—Paf!
> The fast sun sets fast,
> The red sun sets fast.
> They march in the dark night—
> The Red Army marches,
> The Red Army is near—
> They march, they march.
> Who is shooting these bullets
> That fly so far—they can't see them.
> Something flies in the sky
> A fire lights up the sky
> The planes are flying and quickly
> The Red Army came . . .[2]

Children often repeat the first word or words of the first line in the next few lines or in every line of their poems. This repetitiveness lends a songlike rhythm. The following poem was composed by a four-year-old girl:

> There lived a boy young not old,
> There lived a boy made of gold;
> There lived a boy who was never bad
> Who only drank vodka with his dad.

And here is a splendid anapaestic poem by a four-year-old boy who had just learned the meaning of the word "always":

> Let there always be a sky,
> Let there always be a sun,
> Let there always be a mama,
> Let there always be a me.

Repetitiveness is also used to express strong emotion. The above lines express with great conviction the child's indestructible belief in the immortality of all that he loves. One can almost hear in these lines the sturdy voice of this boy, glorifying life which will never come to an end. The first four words in this poem are identical in every line. But more often children repeat the final word or words. Characteristic of this is the delightful poem by young Taniusha Litvinova:

> A wonder city is Moscow!
> An ancient city is Moscow!
> What a Kremlin in Moscow—
> What towers in Moscow!
> There are Englishmen in Moscow!
> And Chinese in Moscow!
> And everyone praises the city of Moscow!

Children's poems have a remarkable graphic quality. It is a pity that we have so little material, so few examples of beginners' poetry. A collection of such poems could be of great value to teachers, critics, children's authors, and even to illustrators of children's books. It could be useful to illustrators because most children's verses are full of imagery; their poems are pictures in poetry—in every line one finds a clear visual image. This is touchingly obvious in the poem by Irina Ivanova who painted, in words, the view from her window during the Russian Civil War [1918–1922] and its destruction:

> The house is in ruins,
> Its roof on the ground,
> And the children play soldiers
> In and around.

To make a careful study of the special aspects of the poetry of the child, we need thousands of samples. I therefore turn again to my readers with an urgent appeal that they send me their children's poetic compositions so that we can commence a thorough study of children's literary creativity.

In the meantime, as "raw material," I am presenting here several poems already sent to me by my readers:

LITTLE RAIN
(by two-year-old Inna)

Little rain, little rain, where were you?
I was outside making the dew.

THE SUN
(by three-year-old Tatia)

Open, open the gates—
The sun is coming up in the sky!

THE BASHFUL LITTLE BEAR
(by four-year-old Olia)

The little bear stands in the nook
Smiling at a little book—
He's ashamed indeed
That he cannot read.

THE OLD MAN
(by five-year-old Irina)

In a poor old village
Lived a poor old man,
He was not strong
To live so long.

IN THE COUNTRY
(same)

The radish is blooming
The drum is booming
And I drink tea
Excessivelea . . .

I include here, for comparison, two poems by six-year-old children:

FROM THE WINDOW

I look out of my window
And see a clear day,

A bit of green willow,
A sail's shadow on the bay.

THE AMAZING LARK

The children went to the park
To take a look at the brook;
They saw on a twig a lark
Singing his riuk-riuk.

Mothers play more than a minor role in the child's development
of a sensitivity to poetry. He receives his first impressions of rhythm
and rhyme when he is still being breast-fed and his mother sings to
him cradle and rocking songs. Looking through my notes, I find the
following entry, made quite long ago.

A four-month-old infant lies on the bed and makes bubbles with
his mouth, and his mother, seized with a sudden ecstasy, smothers
him with kisses and rhapsodizes as follows:

Butsiki, mutsiki, dutsiki,
Rutsiki, putsiki, book!
Kutsen'ki by, tarakutsen'ki,
Putsen'ki by, marabuk!

She had never heard these "words" (all without meaning) before and
had never said them to anyone else. Ordinarily this woman's speech
was dull and banal. And, suddenly, such a festive blossoming of
poetic creativity, such fireworks of ecstatic sounds! And what is most
splendid is that these *"butsiki, mutsiki, putsiki"* form verses and that
they have rhythm and rhyme. An inarticulate, illiterate woman becomes temporarily a poetess. In her entire life she had had no contact
with poetry, yet she spoke to her baby in verse. And responsible for
all this was her four-mouth-old San'ka, lying naked on her bed, making bubbles. She punctuated her *butsiki*'s with repeated hugs and
kisses. I noticed that in moments of demonstrative affection all
mothers make the same gestures. This accounts for the regular
rhythm and pauses in similar maternal "compositions."

A new little shirtie, shirtie, shirtie,
A new shirtie for my wee little boy,
My little baby,
My little darling.

I could hear the wife of the house caretaker chant these endearments
—their apartment was adjacent to mine. It is remarkable that almost
every normal mother is caught up in this sudden passion for rhythmic poetic outpourings, with every violent assault of tenderness.

Among various kinds of ecstatic speech, these maternal outpourings are by no means the least significant, and were we to seek the
first sources of poetry, we would have to admit that the habit of
versifying is inspired in us by our mothers in the period of our
early childhood, before we learn to speak or walk. For, without being aware of it, every mother, with almost every word or gesture, un-
intentionally accustoms her infant to respond to rhythm.

If the title of this book were *From Forty to Seventy,* I would certainly have noted in it that people who have reached this age—
middle-aged or old people—relatively seldom delight in the reading
of poetry. Of course they do not mind reading now and then some of
the work of this or that poet. But it would hardly occur to any of
them to read it daily and for a long time—to get drunk on poetic
harmonies. To some the movies are much dearer; others are drawn
to symphonic music, and still others to painting, or chess, or novels.
And this is quite natural. One cannot expect that poetry be a major
part of the intellectual life of engineers, physicians, mathematicians,
coal miners, or geologists. However, there are millions of human
beings among us, every one of whom, with the rarest exceptions,
ardently loves poetry, gets "drunk" on it, and cannot do without
it. They are—children, especially little ones.

Before and Now

The proper training of young children in poetry is therefore a most
important part of their education. But this is an unplowed field for
our Soviet eductaors because their predecessors, that is, the educators
of earlier times, did not even recognize poetry as a subject matter for
instruction. Children's versifying was regarded then as a foolish
caprice which should not in any way be encouraged. There is much
evidence on record of the contempt with which these verses composed by children were regarded.

A silent, introspective youth entered the Czarkosel'ski high school [one of the most aristocratic schools of the old regime], formerly attended by Pushkin. It soon developed that this boy was a writer of verse. The school director and the boy's teacher were alarmed. The twelve-year-old poet was convicted and punished. But he did not repent and continued to write verse, hiding his lyrics in his sleeve or in his boots. They were triumphantly detected and confiscated and again the culprit was punished.

His name was Mikhail Saltykov. When he had become a recognized writer, he often recalled how that famous school tried to extinguish in him his ardor for poetry. We learn in his autobiography that Saltykov was carefully watched by his teacher of Russian not only for his "poetic activity" but "equally for his reading of books generally"—the very teacher who should have been expected to be delighted with the literary interests of his gifted student.[3]

In those days the Czarkosel'ski high school prided itself on being loyal to "the tradition of Pushkin"; if this school persecuted childish creativity as a forbidden act, what could one expect of the average school of that era, which had no "literary propensity"? There were many gifted children in those days too, but considering the circumstances in which they lived, only a miracle could save their talents from ruin. They were forced to hide this talent as if it were something shameful, as if it were a dread disease. The eleven-year-old Shevchenko,* feeling an irresistible urge to paint, had to conceal himself and his drawings in some tall reeds; it would have gone hard with him had he been discovered by his irascible teacher.

In the literature of the times, as well, the expression of lack of respect for children's creative efforts was a common occurrence. Nikolai Uspenskii tells in one of his humorous stories about some "insignificant" people who were involved in the publication of a "trivial" provincial newspaper. To prove what "drivel" the paper published, the author numbers among its contributors a ten-year-old boy and gives an example, there and then, of the boy's creative writing:

"The sun rose, smiling like a carefree infant playing in its mother's arms." [4]

---

* Taras Shevchenko (1814–1861), son of a serf, was a leading Ukrainian poet, painter, and reformer.

It was typical of this era to consider any literary attempts by children as absurdities.

The author of "Anton Goremyka," D. V. Grigorovich, in his sketch, "Tiresome People," lists various categories of limp and boring types; he does not forget to include among them "all boys from twelve to twenty, inclusive, blessed with some kind of talent." Whether these boys compose verse or draw pictures, they evoke in the writer an irritable boredom, and he considers them on the same level as dunces.

"Such youth," Grigorovich writes sorrowfully, "are appearing in ever larger numbers; they multiply like rabbits. May God grant that the boredom (!) which they inflict in their youthful years be rewarded by something useful in their mature years." [5]

Today such ideas seem to us incomprehensible. We are so used to taking a keen interest in the literary creativity of gifted children that we are incapable of even imagining the yawning fits with which this elderly man of letters was seized when talking about children who wrote or drew.

Another influential writer of the forties and fifties [of the nineteenth century], A. V. Druzhinin, devotes a whole chapter in one of his humorous novels, *Chernoknizhnikov,* to ridiculing a boy who writes poetry. The title of the chapter is, indeed, "The Attempts of a Nine-Year-Old Muse, or an Amazing Tot with Great Hopes."

But today, in the Soviet Union, we have become so used to taking a special interest in the artistic creativity of gifted children that should a child of nine or more, living in faraway Sverdlovsk, for instance, compose several lines about an evergreen tree, the school he attends would, without delay, send these lines to the capital—to the Center for the Education of Children in the Arts. And writers, educators, and journalists would gather around a long table in order to decide a question of more than passing importance: Does this child have talent, and if he has, what means should be taken so that this talent may not be wasted? With feelings of grave responsibility they evaluate every adjective, argue about every line, point out everything that is false and trivial, delight in every shining word. If the truth be told, the works of adult authors are not always studied so devotedly as children's poems and stories.

Eight or nine years ago, about five thousand such manuscripts were sent in to the Center from all corners of the Soviet Union; it had announced to the schools of all the Soviet Republics a country-wide competition for the best artistic writing. I took part in the competition as a member of the jury. The competition was strict and demanding; everything trivial and flat was set aside without compromise, and the prize-winning compositions, although genuinely childish, were fresh and had considerable literary merit.

For instance, there was much freshness and originality in the way Seriozha Orlov (who has since become a professional writer) wrote about the image of a ripe pumpkin:

> It lies there alongside a turnip
> Looking as though it will any moment
> Grunt with contentment
> And wag its tail.

The poems delighted me with their enchanting childishness. The ability of the child to give a dynamic quality to an inanimate object was beautifully revealed in the above poem. With a similar newness of feeling, another schoolboy wrote about his love of a summer landscape:

> And there is enough blueness all around
> To scoop pailfuls of it—and pour it.

Reading the submissions sent to the Center, one is amazed at the diversity of themes. Even an adult poet could envy such variety. There were poems on geology, on Isaac Newton, about a violin virtuoso, about skiing, about the beauty of summer and winter. And about love.

In the past the schools pretended sanctimoniously not to know that adolescents at times fall in love. Love used to be regarded in the school as a shameful, clandestine feeling which one should repress. The love poems submitted in the competition constitute a protest against such an attitude. A young student from Kalinin wrote about parting from a girl he loved:

> A gentle breeze touched
> The green glistening leaves,

> I touched her hand—
> At parting . . .

No one can question the value of our careful and devoted attention to gifted children. However, we must admit that at times it is
too unrestrained. Instead of training young people to take their literary efforts more seriously, and instead of teaching them to set high
standards for themselves, we give them so much encouragement and
praise that some of them, with their noses in the air, begin to regard
themselves as divinely inspired geniuses who do not need to observe
any rules.

Not so long ago, I happened to be visiting a school and was going
up a staircase crowded with students. A young boy wearing a nifty
velvet artist's jacket, pushing his way hard through the crowd,
knocked his violin case against my leg. I scolded him, asking how he
dared push past people that way. He explained, unceremoniously,
and on the run:

"I'm a child prodigy—I'm hurrying to my concert."

To be a child prodigy has become a sort of profession. "I'm a child
prodigy"—these words were said in the same tone as one would say
"I'm a dentist," or "I'm a reporter on the newspaper *Izvestia.*"

The words "talent," "giftedness," are precious, rare, enormously
meaningful words, but some of the bureaucrats of our educational
institutions (alas!—there are still some left!) use every opportunity
to turn them into cheap "nicknames" and to distribute them freely
by means of office slips. It is gratifying and fortunate that those
children who have a genuine artistic promise do not accept such un-
earned glory.

By praising in advance of achievement this or that child who
shows artistic promise, these teachers develop in the child conceit
and presumption, isolate him from his peers, and prepare him for a
life of failure.

Fortunately, this kind of misguidance of children is virtually dis-
appearing right under our eyes. It is enough to read the writings by
children in their own periodicals to become convinced that our
schools have recently had an increasingly beneficial influence on
children's artistic development. Together with a deep appreciation
of the importance of children's creative abilities, leading educators

are now developing proper methods for training children extensively in the writing arts. We notice that some of the leaders of school literary clubs or circles are capable of giving young beginning writers competent and thoughtful help, to equip their talent with a fuller writing technique. But we still have too few such leaders. However, steps are being taken to ensure their increase in number in the future.

There are a few more thoughts I should like to express about the preschool child and poetry. In his third and fourth years, how avidly the child listens to tales in verse, even long ones—three or four hundred lines—and after the third or fourth reading, he already remembers them from beginning to end. Just the same, he demands that they be read to him again and again, several times in a row, reducing to a state of exhaustion his mother or his grandmother, or his kindergarten teacher. Some adults even worry about this: Could not so much poetry burden the child's brain? But for the child this is not a strain, especially since he knows how to manage this load according to his whims or needs. When these poems, absorbed by the child's amazing memory, have played their part in his mental and emotional growth, he "unloads" most of them and retains in his memory only a small part of all the lines that he knew by heart during the age "from two to five."

There is no doubt that the preschool child's own versemaking and his irresistible attraction to poetry—to hear it and memorize it—serve a temporary, soon-to-pass, but very strong need for his mental growth. Those responsible for child training must not neglect to make good use of this "poetic period" in the lives of their young charges, bearing in mind that precisely at this age does poetry serve as the most powerful means of shaping the thoughts and feelings of the child, to say nothing of the way it helps him to orient himself to his language and to enrich his speech. Under the influence of beautiful word sequences, shaped by a pliable musical rhythm and richly melodic rhymes, the child playfully, without the least effort, strengthens his vocabulary and his sense of the structure of his native language.

And if all this is so, those of us who write poetry for young children must apply ourselves seriously to the problem of how best to meet these needs—what form our verses should take, to what aesthetic standards we must adhere—so that they will learn to love our poems and so that these will become near and dear to them. But we will discuss how best to write for the child "from two to five" in one of the chapters to follow—the last one in this book. Right now, that is, in the next chapter, I want to discuss the way children respond to and benefit from nonsense verse.

CHAPTER IV

The Sense of Nonsense Verse

The eye of man hath not heard,
the ear of man hath not seen . . .

WILLIAM SHAKESPEARE, *A Midsummer Night's Dream*

A Letter

I received the following letter:

"Shame on you, Comrade Chukovsky, for filling the heads of our children with all kinds of nonsense, such as that trees grow shoes. I

have read with indignation in one of your books such fantastic lines
as:

> Frogs fly in the sky,
> Fish sit in fishermen's laps,
> Mice catch cats
> And lock them up in
> Mousetraps.

Why do you distort realistic facts? Children need socially useful information and not fantastic stories about white bears who cry cock-a-
doodle-doo. This is not what we expect from our children's authors.
We want them to clarify for the child the world that surrounds him,
instead of confusing his brain with all kinds of nonsense."

As I read this letter I began to feel not only depressed but also
stifled.

What a fusty and hopeless ignorance! This is not a problem that
concerns just me and my modest little poems, but very important
principles governing children's reading materials which cannot be
determined merely on the basis of untutored "common sense," because "common sense" is often the enemy of scientific truth.

I confess that I even pitied my accuser—I felt like taking him by
the hand and leading him out into the sunshine, there to speak to
him from the depth of my heart, without rancor and in the simplest
words, about things he could not understand in the cave of his
narrow-mindedness.

Had he had other resources than "common sense," he would have
realized that the nonsense that seemed to him so harmful not only
does not interfere with the child's orientation to the world that surrounds him, but, on the contrary, strengthens in his mind a sense of
the real; and that it is precisely in order to further the education of
children in reality that such nonsense verse should be offered to
them. For the child is so constituted that in the first years of his
existence we can plant realism in his mind not only directly, by
acquainting him with the realities in his surroundings, but also by
means of fantasy.

Timoshka on a Pussycat

So that my accuser might fully comprehend the above truth, I would converse with him even from a distance and would tell him approximately the following:

Have you noticed, my misguided friend, that in Russian folk rhymes for children—in those masterpieces of poetry which have such great educational power—seldom does anyone gallop on horseback, but more often on a cat or a hen or some other unlikely animal?

> There is thunder in the glen
> As Foma rides a hen;
> Timoshka on a pussycat,
> Fast along the crooked path.

Yes, it seems that there is no bird or animal on which human beings do not take a ride in Russian children's folk verses:

> An old woman mounted a sheep
> And rode up the mountain steep . . .

> Get on a terrier
> Ride to the farrier . . .

> Masha left her hut so narrow
> To take a ride on a tiny sparrow . . .

> Petya holding on to a duck's bill
> Rode out to the field to till . . .

Everywhere in these rhymes there is a distinct departure from the norm—from the horse. How do *you* explain such "nonsense"? Rural youngsters "from two to five" refuse somehow to introduce into their rhymes the horseback rider and his horse. It was only yesterday that they assimilated the important fact that a horse exists for transportation, yet today they knowingly ascribe this function to every unlikely creature.

> Along the stream, along the river
> Mr. Redhead rode a beaver;
> He met Mr. Redface not in a boat
> But riding a silly-looking goat.

Children make every effort to substitute for the horse any kind of nonsensical alternate, and the more palpable the nonsense the more enthusiastically does the children's rhyme cultivate it:

> The cook rode on a rickety van
> Harnessed to a frying pan.

And things are carried so far as to substitute for animals that seem to the child's eye enormous (like horses), microscopic beetles, thus emphasizing even more strongly children's obvious eccentricity in rejecting the normal:

> Tiny children
> On tiny beetles
> Went for a ride.

But it must be noted here that simultaneously with this extreme rejection of the normal, the child is keenly aware of the normal. No matter on what kind of beetles the heroes of these rhymes ride, the child visualizes in his mind the horse that is also present, although invisibly. At times the horse seems to be present visibly, but then it makes its appearance only so that its rejection is even more noticeable:

> I harnessed the horse
> But the horse did not budge;
> I harnessed the gnat
> And the gnat sped away
> To the barn.

This tendency to violate the established order of things is found not only in Russian folklore. For instance, in English children's folk songs we also notice that the motif of horse riding and its variations occur many times: "I'll saddle my cock and I'll bridle my hen"; Jack's mother caught a goose and, mounting its back, she flew to the moon—"Jack's mother . . . caught the goose soon, and mounting its back flew up to the moon. . . ."

At the same time, the English, for centuries a seafaring people, introduced the same custom of turning away from the norm in their verses about sea voyages. The heroes of these verses sail the sea in the most unsuitable vessels: one in a washtub, another in a ladle, and still another in a sieve. Of all the objects in the entire world, the sieve is the least suitable for navigation; it is for this reason that the English folk song makes use of it so readily.

The consistent aversion of the child to carefully established reality is universal. There is no limit to the number of ways the folk rhyme distorts the act of riding on a horse. And even when the horse remains in the verse, other means are used to demonstrate the rejection of the norm. Either the adjectives that always describe the horse and the vehicle it pulls are interchanged:

> He rode on a dappled wagon
> Tied to a wooden horse,

or the rider and the place he rides by are interchanged:

> The village rode
> Past the peasant,

or the rider sits facing in an abnormal direction:

> He sat with his back to the front
> As he rode off to the hunt.

In other words, one way or another, the desired distortion will be achieved, leaving untouched those elements from which the image of the horse rider is formed.

This tendency to present objects in a deliberately incorrect juxtaposition has been borrowed from folk verse and introduced into literary published works, and has been firmly established as a genre in many favorite children's rhymes. For instance, in one such rhyme two mutually exclusive means of transportation appear simultaneously:

> The old woman was riding horseback
> Sprawled in a fine carriage.

Children and "Topsy-Turvies"

There is no doubt that the lines I have just cited have been accepted and approved by countless generations of Russian children. However, although each new generation of parents, grandfathers, and grandmothers sings and recites to children both the good and the inferior, only that which best serves the children's needs and tastes remains in their memories. And when he reaches old age, everyone who heard in his childhood these folk chants passes on to his grandchildren, in his turn, the very best, the most vivid and vital. And everything that is out of tune and incongruous with the psychology of the young child is gradually forgotten and becomes extinct; thus it is not passed on to posterity and ceases to exist for the next generation of youngsters.

This has proven a most reliable method of selection, and, as a result, over the centuries Russian children have inherited a precious treasure of songs which are so superlative because they were, in a sense, perpetuated by the children themselves. What was unsuitable for them perished along a thousand-year-old road. In this way an exemplary children's folklore has come into existence—exemplary in its language and rhythm, as well as ideally suited to the intellectual needs of the young child. Thus it is one of the strongest means of using the greatness of folklore for educational purposes.

The great book that is called by the English *Mother Goose* came into being exactly the same way. The rhymes comprised in *Mother Goose*, called nursery rhymes, had been subjected to the same process of collective selection, unconsciously achieved by a long sequence of generations of children. These verses had been sifted through a thousand sieves before this book came into existence—a book without which one can hardly imagine the childhood years of English, Scottish, Australian, or Canadian children. Many of these rhymes were first published four or five hundred years ago. For instance, "Three Wise Men of Gotham" was already considered an old rhyme in the middle of the fourteenth century.

Why, then, we ask, does one find in these folk verses, so wonderfully adaptable to the education of children, such a large number that are so odd and outlandish and so dedicated to a constant departure from the norm? Why is it that so many typical children's rhymes, approved by millions of youngsters in the course of many centuries, cultivate with such persistence the obvious violation of reality?

I have used only one theme—the horse carrying the man. But if we examine carefully children's folk literature, we find that almost every theme within the ken of children is subjected to the same treatment, as though the idea of a strict order of things and events were intolerable to the three-year-old mind.

Many verses seem to make a special effort to transpose and throw into confusion the many experiences of children which constitute their world. Most often the desired nonsense is achieved by an interchange of the functions of objects. It was by means of this very method that tall tales became part of folklore and are now widely known among Russian children:

> In the sea the corn kiln burns
> While the ship runs in the cornfield.

Six things are combined in these lines in a way that is completely odd: seas and kilns, ships and fields, water and fire. A similar reversed order of typical phenomena of sea and forest is found in English folklore: "The man in the wilderness asked me: 'How many strawberries grow in the sea?' (I answered: 'As many as red herrings grow in the wood.')"

Allow me to repeat and reëmphasize that to be able to respond to these playful rhymes the child must have a knowledge of the real order of things—herrings are in the sea, strawberries grow in the forest. If he does not know, for example, that there is ice only in cold weather, he will not respond to the English verse,

> Three children sliding on the ice
> Upon a summer's day.

It is important first of all to understand and to remember this: all such nonsense verses are regarded by children precisely as nonsense. They do not believe for one moment in their authenticity. The ascribing of incongruous functions to objects attracts them as a diversion.

In the minor Russian genres of folklore this playfulness takes the form of slips of the tongue:

"One and a half milks of jug . . ."

"The belt wears the peasant around its waist . . ."

"Look, the gate barks at the dog . . ."

"The peasant grabbed the dog and beat the stick . . ."

"The dough is kneading the woman . . ."

At times there is an open play on incongruities. An example of this is the following verse which becomes a favorite with every new generation of children:

> The blind man gazes
> The deaf man listens
> The cripple runs a race
> The mute cries: "Help."

Such verses are sometimes called fiddle-faddles or absurdities [*neskladukhi*]:

> Listen, my children
> And I'll sing you a fiddle-faddle:
> "The cow sat on a birch tree
> And nibbled on a pea."

One can cite any number of such *neskladukhi* which testify to the inexhaustible need of every healthy child of every era and of every nation to introduce nonsense into his small but ordered world, with which he has only recently become acquainted. Hardly has the child comprehended with certainty which objects go together and which do not, when he begins to listen happily to verses of absurdity. For some mysterious reason the child is attracted to that topsy-turvy world where legless men run, water burns, horses gallop astride their riders, and cows nibble on peas on top of birch trees.

Isolating these verses in children's folklore as a special category, I have given the whole series the name "rhymed topsy-turvies" [*stishki-pereviortyshi*],[1] and I have tried to ascertain their practical purpose in the context of folk teaching. I said to myself: it is unlikely that the people have so persistently, in the course of so many centuries, offered to new generations of children such a multitude of these odd poetic creations if they did not contribute to their proper psychological development.

Nevertheless, I was unable for a long time to find the reason for the attraction that a topsy-turvy world held for young children. Neither Russian nor foreign authors have written a single word about this. Then, at last, I found the explanation for this strange phenomenon, not in literature, but in life itself.

My two-year-old daughter supplied the answer to this riddle.

For her, at that time, as for many other children of similar age, it was a source of great emotional and mental activity, although in itself seemingly insignificant, that a rooster cries cock-a-doodle-doo, a dog barks, a cat meows.

These simple bits of knowledge were great conquests of her mind. Indelibly and forever did she ascribe to the rooster the "kukareku," to the cat the "meow," to the dog the "bow-wow," and showing off justifiably her extensive erudition, she demonstrated it incessantly. These facts brought simultaneously clarity, order, and proportion to a world of living creatures as fascinating to her as to every other tot.

But, somehow, one day in the twenty-third month of her existence, my daughter came to me, looking mischievous and embarrassed at the same time—as if she were up to some intrigue. I had never before seen such a complex expression on her little face.

She cried to me even when she was still at some distance from where I sat:

"Daddy, 'oggie—meow!"—that is, she reported to me the sensational and, to her, obviously incorrect news that a doggie, instead of barking, meows. And she burst out into somewhat encouraging, somewhat artificial laughter, inviting me, too, to laugh at this invention.

But I was inclined to realism.

"No," said I, "the doggie bow-wows."

" 'Oggie—meow!" she repeated, laughing, and at the same time watched my facial expression which, she hoped, would show her how she should regard this erratic innovation which seemed to scare her a little.

I decided to join in her game and said:

"And the rooster meows!"

Thus I sanctioned her intellectual effrontery. Never did even the most ingenious epigram of Piron evoke such appreciative laughter in

knowledgeable adults as did this modest joke of mine, based on the
interchange of two elementary notions. This was the first joke that
my daughter became aware of—in the twenty-third month of her
life. She realized that not only was it not dangerous to topsy-turvy the
world according to one's whim, but, on the contrary, it was even amusing to do so, provided that together with a false conception about
reality there remained the correct one. It was as if she perceived in
an instant the basic element in comedy, resulting from giving simultaneously to a series of objects an opposite series of manifestations.
Realizing the mechanics of her joke, she wished to enjoy it again and
again, thinking up more and more odd combinations of animals and
animal sounds.

It seemed to me at that point that I understood the reason for the
passion that children feel for the incongruous, for the absurd, and
for the severing of ties between objects and their regular functions,
expressed in folklore.

The key to this varied and joyful preoccupation which has so
much importance in the mental and spiritual life of the child is
play, but play with a special function.

The Educational Value of Topsy-Turvies

Many children's rhymes are the products of games; but topsy-turvies
[pereviortyshi] are a game in themselves.

To all those categories of games about which we have learned so
much in recent times from the writings of D. B. Elkonin, A. P.
Ussova, D. B. Mendzheritskaia, and others (to say nothing of the
works of Gorki and Makarenko), we must add the following category:
mental games and thinking games, because the child plays not only
with marbles, with blocks, with dolls, but also with ideas. No sooner
does he master some idea than he is only too eager to make it his toy.

A most widely used method in these mental games is precisely a
reversal of the normal relationship of things: ascribing to object A
the function of object B, and the other way around. When my two-
year-old daughter forced the imaginary dog to meow, she was playing
this kind of game. To participate in this game, I immediately composed for her a whole series of similar topsy-turvies:

> The piglet meowed—
> Meow! Meow!
>
> The kittens oinked—
> Oink! Oink!
>
> The ducklings clucked—
> Cluck! Cluck! Cluck!
>
> The chickens quacked—
> Quack! Quack! Quack!
>
> The sparrow came skipping
> And like a cow mooed—
> Moo-oo-oo!
>
> The bear came running
> And started to roar—
> Kukareku!

This poem was written as an "order" and as a prescription for the child.

I felt like a carpenter who shaped a toy for his child.

The most important aspect of such toys is that children must invariably regard them as something amusing.

And all rhymes, without exception, adaptable to such games, are in the eyes of children—humorous.

The more aware the child is of the correct relationship of things, which he violates in his play, the more comical does this violation seem to him.

No wonder Kolia Shilov laughed so hard when he managed to twist the familiar phrase about the ringing bells and the flying birds:

"The birds ring, the bells fly!" he said when he was three, and roared with laughter at this peculiar fabrication.

Kolia was only two when he called his uncle "Aunt" and his aunt "Uncle," and he was delighted with his invention:

"Uncle Manya! Uncle Manya!"

The artist Konstantin Kazansky has informed me that his four-year-old daughter sings for hours:

> I'll give you a piece of milk
> And a jug full of silk,

annoying with this her grandmother, who corrects her every time.

The eagerness to play with topsy-turvies is natural to nearly every child at a certain stage of his mental growth. This play may be a gay diversion, but this is not its chief function. In most of their games children are, on the contrary, extremely serious. At this very moment there is a young boy running around under my balcony, with puckered brow—for about two hours now he has appeared in his own eyes as a locomotive. With dogged conscientiousness, as if carrying out some necessary but difficult task, he has been speeding along imaginary rails and panting, hissing, and whistling, and even letting out steam. There has been no laughter whatever in this play in spite of its being one of his favorite games. He has given himself over to it with a stern persistence, making endless journeys between the river bank and his home. While he plays this game his face is a veritable locomotive, and unlike any human face.

If those mental games about which we have been speaking seem to the child comical, this happens first of all because of the reversed juxtaposition of objects, which in itself produces in most instances a comical effect; second, because these games are regarded by the child as nothing but games. Play as it is experienced in any other type of game is accepted by the child voluntarily as self-deception, and the more self-deception is involved, the more attractive is the game. In topsy-turvies the situation is completely opposite—the play is enjoyed to the extent that there is awareness of the self-deception; recognizing this awareness takes first importance.

Of course every illusion must inevitably have some restraints in order that the game be realized as such. When a child bakes sand pies on the beach, he never forgets himself to the point of consuming these delicacies. He is always in control of his illusions and knows perfectly well those limits within which it is important that he hold them. He is the strongest realist in his fantasies. But to the child who plays that he is a locomotive, his game affords greater satisfaction the more he believes in the illusion produced by his imagination. However, to the child who plays with topsy-turvies, in an "upside-down world," this playing affords pleasure only if he does not forget for a single moment the actual juxtaposition or interrelation of things, which is the exact opposite of what happens when he plays other types of games. In other words, the pleasure is the greater the less he believes in the illusion created by his imagination.

When a child intentionally shuffles around the characteristics of the mute and the blind and makes a mute man yell and a blind one see, this game appears to him as a game only because he actually knows and remembers the true characteristics of the mute and the blind. Here he does not give himself up to illusion, but exposes it and thus makes realism triumph.

The recognition of play as play, of course, increases the humor of it, but, I must reiterate, it is not humor that the child seeks when he plays this kind of game; his main purpose, as in all play, is to exercise his newly acquired skill of verifying his knowledge of things. We know that the child—and this is the main point—is amused by the reverse juxtaposition of things only when the real juxtaposition has become completely obvious to him. No sooner, for instance, does he acquaint himself with the most useful truth, that heat burns, than he is ready to derive great fun from the jolly English folk song about a droll person who burned himself with cold porridge.

In this way, this mental game signifies for the child the successful culmination of a certain series of mental efforts which he has made to master his concepts of the world around him.

Let us suppose that a child has firmly acquired the knowledge that largeness goes with strength and smallness with weakness, and that he has established in his mind, permanently, that the bigger the animal, the stronger it is. When this idea of the direct dependence of strength on size is finally very clear to him, the child begins to play around with it. The play consists in substituting for this actual association an opposite one. Thus this game is expressed in countless children's rhymes about the most puny insects to which are attributed the characteristics of enormous beasts. In this way the death of a tiny fly is dramatized as a catastrophe of cosmic dimensions:

> The sea was greatly agitated
> The earth moaned
> As the fly drowned.

The facetious description of the tiny and the lightweight in terms of the huge and the heavy is one of the most widely used types of

topsy-turvies in children's folklore. In an English folk song Simple
Simon casts a fishing rod into a small pail and pulls out a whale. In
another, from the same group, a "squad" of tailors, numbering
twenty-four, sail on a snail and no sooner does the small snail reveal
its horns than they scatter in fright. In this instance the motivation
for this reversed juxtaposition is the cowardice of the tailors. But no
matter what the motivation, the essence of the game is the deliberate
reversing of normal positions, relations, or qualities of things.

Most often this reversing is marked by foolishness; Simon who
tries to fish a whale with a tiny rod is called "simple." No smarter
than the British Simon is our Russian *Motornyi* who eats and drinks
his puttees and swallows his shoes. This perversion of the truth
through stupidity is quite gratifying to the child—he feels an intellectual superiority over those who reveal such profound ignorance
of the surrounding world: "I'm not such a fool as they are." This
childish self-satisfaction is served by all sorts of songs and stories
about simpletons who act contrary to the established order of things:

> No matter what the fool does
> He does it wrong!
>
> [*Chto ni delaet durak,*
> *Vse on delaet ne tak!*]

The function of similar rhymes and stories is obvious; for every
"wrong" the child realizes what is "right," and every departure from
the normal strengthens his conception of the normal. Thus he values
even more highly his firm, realistic orientation. He tests his mental
prowess and invariably he passes this test, which appreciably increases his self-esteem as well as his confidence in his intellectual
abilities; this confidence is most essential to him in order that he
may not become discouraged in his chaotic world. "I'm not the kind
that burns himself with cold *kasha;* I'm not one to get scared of a
snail; I will certainly not look for strawberries on the bottom of the
sea." The main importance in children's play with topsy-turvies lies
in this verifying and self-examination. This is an additional reason
for the joy in topsy-turvies—they raise the child's self-appreciation.
And this is useful because it is essential for the child to have a high
opinion of himself. Not for nothing does he show such avidity for

praise and approval from morning till night, as he boasts about his excellent qualities.

He cannot bear to admit that he is incapable of performing those acts that are performed in his presence by others. No matter what is done in his presence, the two-year-old considers the doer his competitor whom he must surpass. The only reason that children are not disturbed by their incompetence is that they do not suspect the limitations of their competence. And when, on occasion, they become aware of the extent of their inabilities, they are reduced to tears.

The child wants to be the Columbus of all Americas and to discover each one anew for himself. He touches everything, puts everything in his mouth in order to accelerate his acquaintance with the unknown, to learn about the world's affairs and customs, because every lack of understanding, every evidence of ignorance, hurts the child as physical pain does. We would all be great chemists, mathematicians, botanists, and zoölogists by the age of twenty if this burning curiosity about everything that surrounds us did not weaken after we acquired the initial and most essential knowledge for mere survival.

Fortunately, the child does not suspect the enormousness of the incomprehensible that surrounds him. He is always inspired by the sweetest illusions. Which of us has not seen children who are naïvely convinced that they can hunt lions, conduct orchestras, swim oceans, and so forth?

This inquisitive and ambitious explorer of the world must feel great joy when it becomes clear to him that vast regions of knowledge have already been permanently conquered by him, and that errors are made by others but not by him. *Others* do not seem to know that there is ice only in winter, that it is impossible to burn one's tongue with cold porridge, that the cat does not fear mice, that mute people are incapable of crying "Help." *He,* however, has become so sure of these truths that he can even play with them.

When we notice that a child has started to play with some newly acquired component of understanding, we may definitely conclude that he has become full master of this item of understanding; only those ideas can become toys for him whose proper relation to reality is firmly known to him.

Anarchy is unbearable to the mind of the child. He believes that there are laws and rules everywhere and he yearns passionately to discover them; he is disturbed when he observes some unexpected discrepancy.

I remember how sad my three-year-old daughter became when she heard adults say that a large cloud traversed the sky.

"How can a cloud possibly walk when it has no legs?" she asked, almost in tears.

These near tears explained much to me. When a child has only recently concluded, after a strenuous mental effort, that legs are a necessary means for walking and that some adults (naturally, infallible) destroy this generalization with a patently contradictory "fact," again introducing disorder into that region of his knowledge which he has considered free from any chaos, the child is overcome by confusion.

So much confusing and fragmentary knowledge is heaped upon the young child daily that if he did not have this fortunate desire to resolve chaos, he would surely lose his mind by the age of five. Necessity compels him to conduct a tireless classification of all phenomena; it is impossible not to be amazed at the extraordinary skill with which this most difficult task is accomplished and at the delight the child feels at his victory over chaos.

Being an unacknowledged genius of classification, systemization, and coördination of things, the child naturally reveals a heightened interest in those mental games and experiments where these processes are most in use. Hence the popularity of every variety of rhymed topsy-turvies among children down through the centuries.

This nonsense would be dangerous for children only if it obscured from them the authentic and the real interrelations of ideas and things. But not only do topsy-turvies not obscure them, they make them clearer, color them, and underscore them. They strengthen (not weaken) the child's awareness of reality. This gives the nonsense of topsy-turvies its educational value.

Another important essential of the play experience derived from topsy-turvies is that they are by their very nature humorous. No other kind of nonsense verse brings the child so close to the basic elements of humor.

And this is not an insignificant matter—to develop in children a sense of humor; it is a precious quality which will increase the child's sense of perspective and his tolerance, as he grows up, of unpleasant situations, and it will enable him to rise above pettiness and wrangling.

In general, the child has a great need for laughter. To supply him with the right material for the satisfaction of this need is not the simplest problem of child rearing. For this reason I have considered it worth while to devote this special chapter to the analysis of obvious and deliberate nonsense verses in order to prove that even such nonsense verses as seem to have no claim to any kind of educational value—that even they can be highly beneficial, legitimate, and useful.

These rhymes attracted me because they have been held in such contempt for so long a time as being sheer absurdity, and have even been considered harmful; for some time it has been impossible to find any home-grown "Fröbel" * who does not regard it as his duty to protect small children from them.

In the process of rehabilitating these slandered creations of folklore, I have tried, at the same time, to point out the danger in the naïve utilitarian criteria by which, not so long ago, verses for children were judged—criteria that are used even now in many articles and reviews. In considering this question, we have seen convincing proof again and again that untutored "common sense" is an unreliable guide for anyone who seeks scientifically based truth even in matters of literature.

Only when we leave the narrow confines of "common sense" and venture forth into the broad fields of research can we reveal, by means of diligent comparison and analysis, that what untutored "common sense" claims to be thoughtless and harmful must actually be recognized not only as useful but as vitally important.

Although I by no means insist that one has to bring up children exclusively on such nonsense rhymes, I am nevertheless convinced that children's literature from which all "nonsense" is expurgated will fail to meet certain inherent needs of the three- to four-year-old child, and will deprive him of wholesome mental nourishment.

I, at least, do not know a single child who has for a single moment been led into confusion by nonsense verse. On the contrary, it is a

---

* Friedrich Fröbel (1782–1852) was a German teacher and educational theoretician about the preschool child. He created the word "kindergarten."

favorite mental game by which children of this age detect absurdities
and see them in relation to realities. Indeed, these verses are created
for this purpose.

When I begin to read to youngsters my poem about the miracle
tree on which all kinds of footwear grow, I know in advance that
they will most certainly inform me that such trees do not exist and
that shoes, slippers, booties, and rubbers are bought in stores. This
tale amuses them so much because it is so easy to refute it, and thus
the arguments against it become a sort of game by means of which
the children, so to speak, test themselves. For this extremely useful
type of game there exist in children's folklore throughout the world
countless topsy-turvies, almost every line of which represents a violation of the normal relationship between objects.

Do we have the right to banish from child lore the material for
such a beneficial mental exercise?

Soon after I first published my views on this subject, I noticed with
the greatest satisfaction that the term "rhymed topsy-turvies," proposed by me, began to be accepted in the literature on children.[2]
Nevertheless, I was concerned about this question: Was there not
something contradictory between the ideas I put forth and the ideals
and principles of contemporary Soviet culture? Could there be a
serious error in my belief about the beneficial role played by nonsense topsy-turvies and their function in instilling in children correct
notions about the world around them? Recently an authoritative
answer has been given to this question. An eminent Soviet educator,
Professor A. V. Zaporozhets, has expressed with obvious agreement
the basic ideas developed by me in this chapter. He worded his
agreement in the following incontrovertible way: "Children become
so convinced of reality that they begin to enjoy all kinds of topsy-
turvies [*pereviortyshi*]. Laughing at them, the child reveals and deep-
ens his correct conceptions of surrounding reality." [3]

Generally the educational values of nonsense and fabrications
offered in the writings for the older preschool child are manifold, and
disprove the utter absurdity of those crude criteria with which, not so
long ago, the "great literature for the small" was approached in our
country.

We have in Soviet children's literature a splendid poem using this play on topsy-turvies: *What a Scatterbrain!* by S. Marshak.* This poem derives much hilarity from the absurd actions of a man who puts on a shirt for pants, gloves for felt boots, for a hat a frying pan, and so on. Every similar action is caused by his phenomenal absent-mindedness. And the refrain is:

> What a funny scatterbrain
> From the street called Bassain.

This poem has enjoyed tremendous popularity. It was published in the 1920's and has been issued in dozens of editions and translated into almost all languages. Although there has been no Bassain Street in Leningrad for a long time (it was renamed Nekrasov Street), the saying "Scatterbrain from Bassain" has become a national byword and is heard everywhere—in the movies, on streetcars, in clubs:

> "Oh, you scatterbrain from Bassain."
>
> [*"Ekh ty rasseiannyi s Basseinoi."*]

The terse, gay, bright lines of *Scatterbrain* are full of topsy-turvies. Is that not the reason why it has so consistently found favor with millions of young children?

The Ancestors of the Enemies of Nonsense Verse

If we were to consider those crude utilitarian standards that so-called critics of all shades and hues have until recently applied to the literature for the young, we would have to abolish not only topsy-turvies but, in general, all the best works of folk poetry most loved by children.

This is what was actually done by the misguided "educators" of all lands in the course of centuries—they jealously extirpated this "balderdash and rubbish." But the children proved to be the stronger: they withstood over the centuries the onslaught of "wise" teachers and parents who considered it their moral duty to isolate the young from similar "nonsense."

---

*Samuel Marshak (1887–1964) was an outstanding Soviet lyric poet, children's author, and translator.

Many teachers and parents lacked the patience to wait until the proper age to share with the child the information that was in those times considered most useful for adults. In England, in the sixteenth century, there was a William Copland who prepared for three-year-old children a highly beneficial book, *The Secrets of the Mysteries of Aristotle,* and recommended it as "very good." [4]

One can imagine with what contempt this Copland would regard any "eccentric" who dared to mumble that for children the most nonsensical rhyme about strawberries at the bottom of the sea was more useful than all the Aristotles.

Another children's author of the sixteenth century, Wynkyn de Worde, actually entitled his book *Wyse Chylde of Thre Year Old,* in which, by the way, he addressed to the three-year-old reader the following question:

"By what miracle did the Lord create the heavens?"

Children's authors of those times despised the "child" in children. Childhood seemed to them some kind of an indecent sickness which one had to cure promptly and at any cost. They tried to make a somber adult out of every child.

This is the reason why, until relatively recently, there has not been a single happy book in children's literature anywhere in the world. To laugh with the child was considered degrading by children's authors. Chaucer himself, a genius as a storyteller, when he became a children's writer, composed for his young son *A Treatise on the Astrolabe*—a most protracted and boring piece of writing. This is comparable to feeding an infant beefsteak instead of mother's milk.

The effort on the part of adults to burden the child with their adult experiences is especially noticeable in those periods of history when it seemed to adults that they were in possession of some single secret for salvation, that the "beefsteak" with which they were satisfying their "hunger" at the time was the only wholesome food for everybody.

For this reason, during the domination of puritanism, every children's author tried to make the child the most saintly miniature of Cotton Mather. The only books considered suitable in those days for three-year-olds were funereal discourses on death! A typical child's book of the times was *A Portent for Children,* "about the painless and radiant demise of many pious infants beloved by God"! Such a verse as "Precautions for a Good Little Girl" was considered extremely enlightening and valuable. Here is a faithful translation of it:

> I know, looking into the glass,
> That I am a very pretty lass;
> And that God has given me a lovely body;
> But it is bitter to learn
> That in hell it is doomed to burn.

And here is a poem by John Bunyan, the famous author of *Pilgrim's Progress,* who is known to Soviet readers mainly through the excerpt translated by Pushkin. Bunyan composed for children a very edifying book with the title, *Divine Emblems or Temporal Things Spiritualized.* As an example I have translated from this book the following lines about the frog:

> The cold and wet frog—
> With mouth wide and gluttonous belly
> Sits, shamelessly ugly,
> Croaking like a bloated boaster.
>
> You hyprocrites resemble it fully—
> You are just as cold, arrogant, and mean,
> And your mouth is as wide,
> Insulting the good and praising evil . . .

Similar poems were considered by bigots of those days to be, without question, ideal for children, and were highly recommended.

The only emotion that the books of those times sought to evoke in children was terror. Here are some dialogues that were included in an American Puritan publication, *The First Reader:*

"Will you be content in hell?"

"No, I will be tortured terribly."

"And with whom will you have to live there?"

"With legions of devils and millions of sinners."

"Will they console you?"

"No, they are quite likely to increase my torments."

"If you are sent to hell, will you suffer there a long time?"

"Forever." [5]

Thomas White, a Protestant minister, advised English children in
A Little Book for the Little (1702):

"Read no ballads, no foolish fantasies, but only the Bible and
also a very easy and pious book, *Plain Man's Pathway to Heaven.*
Read also *The Lives of the Martyrs,* who died in the name of
Christ. Read more often Discourses on Death, about the tortures
of Hell, about the awful Judgment and the Agony of Jesus Christ." [6]
He goes on to narrate soul-rending stories about the Martyrs—one
had his head chopped off, another was cooked in boiling water, another had his tongue cut out, and a fourth was thrown to the tigers.
White wrote about all these mutilations and tortures with a relish
that makes one suspect him of being a sadist.

Even later, however, when the Puritan yoke was lifted, "amusing
stories, rhymes, puns" continued to be regarded as vicious, although
for different reasons.

Adults were drawn to science and, of course, they were anxious
to convert every child immediately into a scientist. The Industrial
Revolution had begun and the spokesman for utilitarianism, John
Locke, soon began, by degrees, to train children for this orientation.
The slogan for education became: to enrich the child's mind as soon
as possible with the most useful scientific information—in geography,
history, mathematics; down with everything childish, or inherently
for children, like games, rhymes, amusements! Children need only
that which is adult, learned, generally useful. In accord with Locke's
principles, adults succeeded in working on the poor children in such
a way that by the age of five they could point out any country on
the globe.

Unfortunately, by the age of ten many of the miniature Lockes
became idiots. It is not hard for one to become an idiot when he is
robbed of his childhood!

For Locke childhood was a mistake of nature, a universal disorder,
an oversight by the Creator. This mistake had to be rectified and the
sooner the better! If it is forever impossible for children to be born
omniscient Lockes, let us make them into Lockes in the shortest
time—by the fifth or sixth year of their life! Naturally, as a result
of this presumptuous attitude toward the real needs and tastes of
children, Locke condemned without mercy all existing children's
books, ballads, poetry, fantasies, fairy tales, proverbs, and songs which,

in his opinion, were bad because they were neither geography nor algebra. All of children's literature, vital to the child as air, Locke called triviality, labeling it without hesitation "a useless trumpery," and recommending for children's reading only one book—Aesop's.[7]

It took hundreds of years for grownups to realize that children have the right to be children. Slowly the child won respect for himself and for his games, interests, and tastes. Finally it began to be understood that if a three-year-old child who received a globe refused to hear about continents and oceans but preferred to spin this globe, to turn this globe, to catch this globe, it meant that he needed not a globe but a ball. Even for their mental (to say nothing of physical) development, three-year-old children could benefit more from a ball than from any globe of the world.

But when it came to childrens' books or verses, the educators of the time stubbornly discarded everything genuinely childish, everything that seemed to grown-up minds unnecessary and senseless.

It is characteristic of such an attitude that even at the present time the English provincial mentality, in proportion to its lowering of standards, increasingly feels ashamed of the great and bold poetic fantasies inherited from its ancestors. In revising *Mother Goose,* for instance, an attempt has been made to adjust the rhymes to its trivial and dull ideas. Recently I came across one edition of this classic in which the most saucy verses were so consistently flattened out that they resembled Sunday hymns. The famous "Hey, diddle diddle" about the cow that jumped over the moon and the dog that laughed (like a human being) was redone by some sober "parson" as follows: the dog does not laugh but barks, the cow does not jump over the moon but under the moon, that is, below, in the meadow.[8]

Just a few words have been changed and the book has become quite sensible; in fact, it has only one fault: nothing would induce a child to love it or to sing its lines. And the "senseless" version, the "illegal" and banished one, has existed for four hundred years and will survive (precariously) another thousand, because it represents the means by which the child confirms for himself the authentic and actual interrelationship of objects and creatures.

This battle against the fantasy in these genuine verses is carried on by English provincialism, with equal success, via a whole series of illustrations and drawings for these rhymes. For instance, for the rhyme about Humpty-Dumpty-who-sat-on-the-wall, a picture was provided showing not a broken egg but an ordinary boy sitting on a wall and holding a nest. The nonsense verse about children skating on ice on a hot summer's day was illustrated by a winter scene with children in fur jackets skating on ice on a frosty winter's day.

The present-day inhabitant of England seems to be ashamed of those wonderful books that he has inherited from his forefathers; he is using all available means to spoil them. And he is succeeding.

In the Soviet Union we now treat with respect and care not only children's folklore but everything else that represents the creative genius of the people. If any editor of an anthology of children's folklore dared now to distort the original text—this would be considered sacrilegious. All kinds of puns, riddles, taunts, counting rhymes, and cradle songs now surround children from their infancy, since the oral folk tradition is being perpetuated in the child's world of today by means of printed collections of these masterpieces of folk creativity, published yearly by the State Publishing Bureau of Children's Books (Detgiz) and by many regional publishing establishments; to say nothing about the folk tales produced by all the various peoples of our country, especially Russian folk tales. They are being issued in such huge yearly "harvests" that it is impossible to imagine a single kindergarten or a single literate family where there are children without these books.

All this is, of course, splendid! This is a great victory for the vanguard of educators over the leftist pedagogues who had, with stupid persistence, banished our great and poetic folklore from the educational experience of Soviet children.

The victory is great but, unfortunately, not complete. It is as if the victors do not quite believe that they *are* victors. At times they seem to quail even within the domain they have conquered, to act with hesitation, looking around for danger signals. One would think that they, too, are afraid that fairy tales or rhymed topsy-turvies might cause harm to the materialistic world outlook to which the adult citizen must, in the last analysis, be brought by the entire system of education in our country.

The intellectual timidity of these people consists in their classifying the whole wealth of nonsense verse and rhymed topsy-turvies, from both folklore and nonfolklore sources, as merely an "amusing" genre of children's literature.

They refer to them, indeed, as gay, humorous, amusing rhymes. And they say condescendingly: "Well, after all, it is not a sin for children to laugh, let's read to them, for the sake of laughter, some of these diverting nonsense rhymes."

However, it is high time to promote these "nonsense" verses into the category of educationally valuable and perceptive works of poetry which contribute to strengthening in the child's mind the correct understanding of reality.

Of course, the reading of topsy-turvies, tall tales, fairy tales, and fantasies to children is only one way of achieving this goal; this way must not be isolated from many others. But it is necessary to use it with assurance, with energy, and with courage, remembering that this is not a children's diversion—not merely a diversion, that is— but a most useful mental effort, as we have seen. With the help of fantasies, tall tales, fairy tales, and topsy-turvies of every type, children confirm their realistic orientation to actuality.

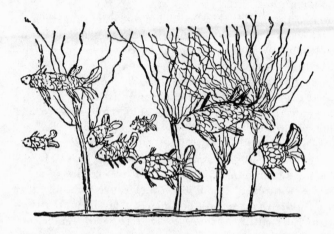

CHAPTER V

The Battle for the Fairy Tale

THREE STAGES

A Discussion about *Munchausen* (1929)

It happened in Alupka [in the Crimea] in 1929. The sick children in the sanatorium were exhausted and restless from the sweltering heat. They were noisy and whiny, and a listless, slovenly-looking woman was clucking over them, henlike, without managing to quiet them down.

I had come there that day from far away. To cheer them up I began to read to them *Baron von Munchausen*.

Within several minutes they were "neighing" with pleasure. Listening to their happy giggles I realized for the first time so fully what an appetizing treat this book is for nine-year-old youngsters, and how much duller would be the lives of many children if this book did not exist in the world.

I continued to read the story with the most tender feelings of gratitude to the author, relishing the hearty laughter of my listeners as I read on about the hammer that flew to the moon, the journey on the cannon ball, the horse's legs that were put out to pasture. And whenever I paused for breath the children cried: "Go on! Go on!"

Well, that same slovenly-looking woman came running up to me—she was no longer listless—she seemed upset and there were red spots of anger all over her face.

"What's this?" she snapped. "What do you think you're doing? We never . . . it's out of the question!"

She snatched the book out of my hand and looked at it as if it were a frog. She carried it off holding it gingerly with two fingers, while the children howled with disappointment and while I followed after her in a state of mild shock. For some reason my hands were shaking. . . .

Then there appeared a young man in some kind of uniform and both began to speak to me as if I were a thief whom they had caught red-handed:

"What right do you have to read this trash to our children?"

And the young man went on to explain, in an instructor's tone, that books for Soviet children must be not fantasies, not fairy tales, but only the kind that offer most authentic and realistic facts.

"But, please consider," I tried to argue, "that it is indeed through its fantasy that this fairy tale emphasizes to the children reality. Their very laughter at every adventure of Munchausen testifies to their awareness that he is fabricating and telling ridiculous falsehoods; that is why they laugh—because each time they counterpose reality to his wild imaginings. This is their contest with *Munchausen*—a contest from which they invariably emerge victorious. This is what pleases them most of all because it enhances their self-appreciation. 'So you wanted to fool me? Well, you've got the wrong fellow!' This is what each of them says to himself. The children carry on this argument with the author, and their weapon is realism. Go and ask your children whether they believed a single word of Munchausen's tale. Don't be surprised if they laugh right in your face.

"And you insult them with your wild fear that *Munchausen* will stupefy them! Is this not a mockery of nine-year-old citizens of the Soviet land, to consider them unenlightened dunces who will believe that a hammer can fly to the moon?"

The eyes of the two pedagogues were stony. But I could not give in:

"Or is it that you are afraid that the buffoonery of Munchausen will stimulate in the children a feeling of humor? Why is it that a gay book fills you with such revulsion, as if you were gravediggers or professional mourners? Or is it that you are trying to instill in them a violent dislike for books? Well, I can assure you that you will succeed in this because you are on the right track! And, believe me, those educators who are true champions of improved education for Soviet children will laugh at you and judge you. . . ."

I waited for their objections; but these individuals were of that breed of unthinking people who seem to be insulted when invited to think for themselves. Only one of them, highbrowed and sullen, spoke up, saying peremptorily that my opinions were "Chukovsky-isms."

And thus ended our discussion. The children were saved from Munchausen. I threw my traveling bag over my shoulder and went out into the hot Crimean sunshine.

In this bag I carried my beloved *Gulliver, The Fairy Tales of the Brothers Grimm, The Little Humpbacked-Horse;* I had wanted to leave these as gifts for the sick children, but the highbrowed one had looked through them and pushed them away with a bored air, saying:

"These are of no use to us. We would rather have books about diesels and radio."

Walking along the shore, on a stone path, I kept thinking about what had just happened.

Why are these peculiar people so convinced, I thought to myself, that radio and *The Little Humpbacked-Horse* are so incompatible? Why do they think that if a child reads this fairy tale he will most certainly turn away from technology and will henceforth daydream about firebirds to the end of his days? How did they arrive at this categorical position—either the fairy tale or the dynamotor? As if the most uninhibited fantasy and imagination were not needed for the inventing of the dynamotor! Fantasy is the most valuable attribute of the human mind and it should be diligently nurtured from earliest childhood, as one nurtures musical sensitivity—and not crushed. Lenin had said about fantasy: "It is incorrect to think that fantasy is useful only to the poet. This is an insipid prejudice! It is useful even in mathematics—even differential and integral calculus could not have been discovered without it. Fantasy is a quality of the highest importance." [1]

Charles Darwin was such a fantasy spinner in his childhood that everyone thought him to be a worse fibber than Munchausen.

All these arguments seemed to me so conclusive that I felt like returning at once to the scene of my "defeat" to prove to the high-browed one that he was irreparably crippling the children in his care by banishing fairy tales from their reading.

Very early the next day I appeared before him and offered him my thoughts on the subject and, in conclusion, I reached into my traveling bag, took out a certain book, and read from it the following words:

"We should develop the child's imagination, or, at least, we must not inhibit its natural development. In this connection, the reading of fairy tales is very important for little children. We often meet parents these days who are against fairy tales. They do not make them available to their children, seeking to bring up sober, practical individuals. I always say to such parents that their children will never become mathematicians or inventors. . . ."

The highbrowed one reached for his cap.

"And do you know who wrote these words?" I asked him. "This was written not by some poet or storyteller but by a professor of applied mechanics, the author of the books, *The Elements of Statics* and *A Course in the Resistance of Materials*—books that have taught whole generations of outstanding Russian scientists. At the end of his distinguished career in teaching and in science he was convinced that the fairy tale had been his ally and not his enemy, that the engineer who was not brought up in his childhood on fairy tales would hardly become a creative engineer. This scholar's article on the subject was, indeed, entitled, 'The Importance of Fantasy to the Engineer.' [2] Read it and you will see for yourself that the fairy tale does not interfere with technological education of children but, on the contrary, helps it."

But the highbrowed one pushed away this book, too.

"Don't you want to read it?" I asked. "Why not?"

"Because today is my day off," he answered with an air of self-importance.

Fortunately, there were others at this sanatorium, young and fine-spirited teachers; they supported me wholeheartedly. But their efforts did not save Munchausen!

For the highbrowed one had received his education in Kharkov, where a certain brand of pedologist * was firmly entrenched at the time. These "experts" were miserable theoreticians of child guidance, contending that fairy tales, toys, and songs were useless to children of proletarians. The highbrowed one, thanks to this group of overpersuasive specialists, felt himself completely freed from the obligation to think for himself.

I found out later that A. S. Makarenko † wrote with indignation about this breed of pedologists:

"I always tried honestly to grasp the pedological 'theory,' but, from their very first words, my brain became strained and I did not even know how to define this entire doctrine: as the rantings of madmen, as a deliberate intention to harm children, as a devilish Homeric mockery of our entire society, or merely as an example of ordinary stupidity. I could not understand how it could happen that the tremendously important problem of the education of millions of children, that is, millions of future citizens—Soviet workers, engineers, military, agronomists—was decided by an obscurantist clique and right before everyone's eyes." [3]

My *Munchausen* became the victim of a similar clique.

"There Is No Such Thing as a Shark"

Once upon a time there lived in Moscow a pedologist by the name of Stanchinskaia. And a very strange thing happened to this pedologist.

She was also a mother, and she did everything in her power to protect her son from fairy tales. Even when she talked to him about animals she made sure to mention only those he had seen with his

---

* A pedologist is an authority on children's education, psychology, and culture.

† Anton Makarenko (1888–1939), an outstanding Soviet educator and writer, founded the theory of education to mold "the Soviet Man."

own eyes. After all, he had to grow up a realist! The fewer harmful fantasies the better! She considered especially harmful fairy tales that told about supernatural transformations—werewolves, Baba-Yagas, and others.

This ardent foe of the fairy tale even published an article in a Moscow magazine in which she wrote: [4]

"We propose to replace the unrealistic folk tales and fantasies with simple realistic stories taken from the world of reality and from nature."

No compromises, no weakening! Let us get rid of all fairy tales, epic tales, the entire folklore of Russia and of the rest of the world—without any exception! And everything would have been just fine, but, unfortunately, as a loving mother she began to keep a most detailed diary about her little son. Without being aware of it, she contradicted, in her entries, all her favorite arguments about the harmful influences of fantastic tales and destroyed with her own pen, so to speak, her formidable theories.

She wrote in this diary—and it has been published—that her boy, as if to make up for the fairy tales of which he had been deprived, began to spin from morning till night the wildest fantasies. He pretended that a red elephant came to live in his room; he invented a friend—a bear whom he named Cora; and he would often say, "Please, don't sit on the chair next to mine because—can't you see? —the she-bear is sitting on it." And, "Mother, why are you walking right on top of the wolves?! Can't you see the wolves standing there?" [5]

And with the first snow he became a reindeer, a little reindeer in a Siberian forest. And if he sat on a rug, the rug would immediately be transformed into a ship. At any time, with the power of his childish fantasy, he could draw any animal out of the air. His mother wrote in the diary:

"Today he returned home carrying something very carefully:

" 'Mommie, I brought you a little tiger,' and he extended to me his empty hand. 'Do you like my baby tiger?'

" 'Yes, yes, my little one!'

" 'Let him stay with us,' he pleaded.

"Before sitting down to dinner he placed next to his plate a smaller one, and when his food was brought to him he said:

" 'And for the baby tiger?'

"Once he recounted in a lively manner:

" 'I went down into the sea and splashed about for a while. Then, suddenly, a big tiger came. I hid myself under the shore, then I threw out a net and caught a fish.'

" 'Where is the fish?'

" 'I ate it up—rawl' [6]

"Most of his days were spent this way. Every minute he made up some fairy tale for himself:

" 'Mother, I'm a little bird and you're a bird too. Yes?' [7]

" 'Mother, a bug came to visit me. He wanted to shake hands with me and put out his little paw. . . .' " [8]

And although his mother observed that he literally bathed in fantasies as in a river, she continued to "protect" him from the ill effects of books of fairy tales.

As if there were a basic difference between the fairy tale that a child made up himself and one that was created for him (as a folk tale) by imaginative folk or by a good writer. It makes no difference whether or not the child is offered fairy tales for, if he is not, he becomes his own Andersen, Grimm, Ershov. Moreover, all his playing is a dramatization of a fairy tale which he creates on the spot, animating, according to his fancy, all objects—converting any stool into a train, into a house, into an airplane, or into a camel.

I knew a little boy who seriously warned people when he played chimney sweep:

"Don't touch me! You'll get dirty!"

And another child who, in the course of playing, turned himself into a meat cake and was carefully frying himself in a pan, pushed his mother away from him when she threw her arms around him and covered him with kisses:

"How dare you kiss me—a hot and fried one?!"

No sooner did my three-year-old Mura at play spread her books in a row on the floor than they became a river in which she caught fish or washed clothes. And when she accidentally stepped on one of the books, she exclaimed most convincingly, "Oh, I got my foot all wet!" She sounded so earnest that for a moment I believed it and rushed to her with a towel.

In all this children become authors of and, at the same time, actors in fairy tales, expressing themselves in dramatic play. And their urge to believe in their imaginings is so strong that every attempt to put them into a frame of reality evokes a vigorous protest. I remember, for instance, when three-year-old Bubu surrounded himself with building blocks and declared that this was a zoo:

"I can't, I'm locked in!" he answered when he was invited to go for a walk.

"Come on, walk through the blocks," it was suggested. But this proposed violation of the story he invented offended him to the point of tears. He remained obstinately inside his voluntary prison and agreed to emerge from it only when a block was moved in his construction so as to make it seem like a gate.

Children with a very pronounced sense of fantasy at times push make-believe to the point of eccentricity. Two-year-old Levik, sitting astride the back of his father's neck, loved to conduct a search for himself in the most unlikely places:

"Under the lamp? No! In the thimble? No! In the jug?" and so on.

"Then where is Levik?"

"He's lost! Maybe he is inside a cigarette!" [9]

Once, at play, Natasha played the part of a soldier's wife who, presumably, remained at home and kept house. In the course of the play someone came running with the news that her husband was killed at the front. Natasha sobbed and sobbed. The other children tried to calm her. They assured her again and again that Boria, the child who played the role of her husband, was quite alive. She continued to weep and was not yet quite consoled even at bedtime. That night she moaned in her sleep and when her parents tried to console her, she said:

"So what, if Boria is alive—but they killed my husband!"

Some children were playing Sleeping Beauty; their attention was soon diverted to something else and they left the Princess sleeping on a shelf.

"Come to dinner!" her grandmother called to her.

"I can't. I'm the Princess. I'm asleep."

Not only games, but even the simplest conversations of small children testify to the fact that it is normal for them to regard the world in a fantastic way:

"And the alarm clock never sleeps?"

"Doesn't the needle hurt the stocking?"

And it is this professional storyteller whom we try to protect from the fairy tale by which he lives and breathes!

Fortunately, we may never succeed in this. For, to safeguard his psyche, the child goes "underground" with his fairy tale and makes use of it "illegally," smuggling it into his world.

The well-known children's author, T. A. Bogdanovich, was brought up by another children's author, Aleksandra Annenskaia. Under the influence of the "enlightenment" of the sixties [of the nineteenth century], she so zealously protected the little girl from the *skazka* [the folk tale] that she even hesitated to hire a *niania* * for her, fearing that the nurse would tell the child fairy tales. Only educational books were read to the child—mainly books on botany and zoölogy. But, at night, when the governess finally fell asleep, the child, at last free from the constant supervision, filled her room with all kinds of creatures. Monkeys scampered all over her bed. A fox and her babies suddenly appeared on her table. Strange birds nested in her clothes left folded near her bed, and she talked to these visitors for a long time.

She talked to them because every normal child talks to all creatures and objects and all creatures and objects seem to the child to speak to him. This nightly indulgence in fantasy and her nocturnal exis- tence among imaginary animals gave the little girl immeasurable pleasure, because thus she satisfied a healthy and normal aspect of a child's nature. This child asserted her rights instinctively—her rights to the fairy tale—secretly giving herself up to that fantasy from which her adults shielded her as from typhus. All that her governess accomplished was to send the fairy tale underground and thus give it a much greater charm. Would it not have been better merely to read *Cinderella* or *Little Red Riding-Hood* to this child?

We have seen in an earlier chapter what a five-year-old child did when a too-clever Moscow mother (also an educator by profession), wishing to accustom him to the verities of life, told him too soon about the conception and birth of babies. After listening to her lecture, he at once changed the scientific facts to suit himself and

---

* A *niania* is a simple woman, usually of the peasant class, who is hired to take care of children.

told her that when he was inside her body he played in a little garden and drank tea with an uncle [*diadia*] who sojourned there, and that he saw there, as well, some salesmen selling all sorts of things.

This is what a five-year-old youngster did with the strictly scientific facts which were supplied to him too soon. He thus practically told his mother: "You can see for yourself that right now I need, not a lecture on embryology, but a fairy tale, so as to spend this most important period of my psychological development in a fuller, more marvelous, more sumptuous way. Don't be in too much of a hurry to condition me to adult thinking because every one of your adult truths, according to my nature, I shall, without delay, transmute into fantasy and shall scatter some sand, shall cultivate a garden, and shall set up a counter with salesmen behind it—even in your womb."

Deprived of the folk tale, of a Pushkin fairy tale, or a fairy tale written by a good contemporary poet, children are forced to rely on their own spontaneous compositions.

Deprived of *Munchausen, Gulliver, The Little Humpbacked-Horse,* the young child unconsciously compensates for this loss with countless "do-it-yourself" fairy tales. Therefore, the pedologists who snatched from him folk tales and fairy tales written by the great and the good writers, actually robbing him, committed this robbery without reflection and without, fortunately, even fulfilling their purpose.

The fairy tale continued to flourish in the child's world, except that instead of a folk tale or a tale by Pushkin, or a fairy tale by some living author, the children were obliged to serve themselves with their own fortuitous literary handiwork. Until recently, those in charge of setting standards for children's literature have given insufficient thought to children's demonstrated preference for fairy tales and to the value of such tales in developing, strengthening, enriching, and directing children's capacity for creative thinking and imaginative responses—a value that has been tested by classic works produced over the centuries.

Meanwhile, in our time, after witnessing the realization of the most amazing scientific and social "fantasies" which not so long ago seemed like senseless fairy tales, we must develop a generation of inspired creators and thinkers everywhere, in all fields of endeavor—in science, technology, agronomy, architecture, politics.

Without imaginative fantasy there would be complete stagnation
in both physics and chemistry, because the formulation of new
hypotheses, the invention of new implements, the discovery of new
methods of experimental research, the conjecturing of new chemical
fusions—all these are products of imagination and fantasy.

The present belongs to the sober, the cautious, the routine-prone,
but the future belongs to those who do not rein in their imagination.
Not without reason did the famous British physicist, John Tindale,
champion fantasy:

"Without the participation of fantasy," he wrote, "all our knowledge about nature would have been limited merely to the classification of obvious facts. The relation between cause and effect and
their interaction would have gone unnoticed, thus stemming the
progress of science itself, because it is the main function of science
to establish the link between the different manifestations of nature,
since creative fantasy is the ability to perceive more and more
such links." [10]

Why, then, did our pedologists make the word "fantasy" a word of
derision? In the name of what did they expunge it from the psyche
of young children? In the name of realism? But there are different
types of realism. There is the realism of a Bacon, or a Gogol, or a
Mendeleev,[*] or a Repin [†]—and there is the realism of a teapot, a
roach, or a 10-kopeck piece. Is it to advance the latter type of realism
that we have taken such pains? And does it not seem that the actual
name for this is—Philistinism? We must face the fact that many of our
young children are even at present surrounded by Philistinism. We
have not yet saved them entirely from the pettiness of narrow-mindedness. There are many among our children who are even more
"adult" and more "practical" than their elders; and if we are to save
them from anything, it is precisely from this horrible practicality
instilled in them by old-fashioned and commonplace attitudes.

But the pedologists are worried and tremble at the thought that
children will actually believe that shoes grow on trees. Some children

---

[*] Dmitri Ivanovich Mendeleev (1834–1907), celebrated Russian chemist who
was the first to classify fifty chemical elements and to foresee the existence of at
least forty more.

[†] Ilya Yefimovich Repin (1844–1930), the most renowned Russian painter of
the nineteenth century.

are so suspicious of everything—even the most poetic, that is, the most unreal—that everything beyond the limits of the everyday and the ordinary they consider a bold-faced and senseless fabrication. For instance, once when someone tried to talk to a group of school children about sharks, one of them cried out:

"There is no such thing as a shark!"

Such children know of nothing rare or marvelous on the face of the earth; they know only of bread and cabbage, boots and rubles. To fear that some little fairy tale will turn them into romantics, into incompetents for practical living—this fear can possess only those bureaucratic contrivers who, attending meetings from morning till night, never see a live child.

Protecting little ones from folk songs, tall tales, fairy tales, these people are hardly aware of the banal fetish they make of practicality. As a result, they look upon every children's book as something that must immediately produce some visible, touchable, beneficial effect, as if a book were a nail or a yoke. They thus reveal the pettiness and the narrowness of their Philistine thinking. Their inventions about the harm of fairy tales are in themselves an insane fairy tale which overlooks all concrete facts. This is the only kind of fairy tale that we need to combat—the fairy tale of regressive pedologists about the fairy tale.

And we must say to these mystics: "Stop raving, get down to earth, become realists, look at the actual facts and you will cease trembling before Tom Thumb and Puss in Boots. You will see that by a certain age the fairy tale no longer charms the child so much (provided he lives in a healthy environment), and he then enters upon a period when he relentlessly "exposes" fantasy.

"But how could the Snow Maiden breathe if she had no lungs?"

"How could Baba-Yaga fly in the air on a broom if it had no propeller?"

The fairy tale has now accomplished its task. It has helped the child orient himself to the surrounding world, has enriched his spiritual life, has made him regard himself as a fearless participant in imaginary struggles for justice, goodness, and freedom; and now, when his need of the fairy tale has ended, the child himself does away with it.

But up to the age of seven or eight, the fairy tale is for every normal child the most wholesome food—not just a tidbit but his nourishing daily bread, and no one has the right to deprive him of this health-giving, irreplaceable food.

Formerly, it was precisely this kind of deprivation of the child which pedologists practiced. Not only did they take away from him the fairy tales of Pushkin and Ershov's *The Little Humpbacked-Horse,* and *Ali-Baba,* and *Cinderella,* but they demanded of us writers that we become their collaborators in this evil and senseless deed. And, of course, there were potboiling hacks who, to please the editors, diligently degraded in their writings the fairy tale and in every way mocked its wonders. This was done in the following pattern: a sly, inflexible boy was depicted, to whom all fairy tales were poison. A fairy would appear and would spread before him a magic carpet. But he—

> His hands
> In his pants
> He thrust,
> Snickered,
> Whistled,
> And said:
> "Auntie, you're fibbing—
> And how!
> Who needs you now
> And your magic rug?
> No one can you now fool
> With this or any humbug . . ."

And when someone told him the story of the ubiquitous *Hump-backed-Horse,* he again thrust his hands into his pockets and answered with equal depravity:

> Well, *I* find more jolly
> A long ride on a trolley.

The ill-bred, insolent urchin enjoyed the full admiration of the author.

There were many similar books, and one cannot claim that they did not influence children. Fortunately, not many were thus crippled. The large majority of four-year-old children saved their normal childlike psyche from these despoilers of childhood by means of their own imaginary games and their own fairy tales.

It does not follow from what I have just defended that I yearn for nothing else than that Soviet children should be bemused from morning till night by fairy tales. It is a matter of proportion, strictly observed. But we must not permit petty utilitarian theories of these wretched pedologists to deprive Soviet children of one of the greatest heritages of classical world folklore.

The dynasty of the above-mentioned defenders of the realistic education of children proved to be quite short-lived. In Moscow and in Leningrad and in other major cities there appeared a whole cohort of ardent defenders of the fairy tale, inspired and led by Maxim Gorki. The attackers retreated, not undamaged, and there came a time when everyone thought that they had disappeared forever.

It Was Time To Get Wise (1934)

There were many reasons for this illusion. As early as 1934, especially after the memorable appearance of Gorki at the First All-Union Congress of Soviet Writers, there appeared everywhere repentant educators, editors, and supervisors of kindergartens who had previously participated in the siege against the fairy tale with as much zeal as they were now showing in defending it. At that time the Young Guard Publishing House, and later the Children's State Publishing Bureau, began to put out huge editions of *Hiawatha, The Little Humpbacked-Horse,* and *Munchausen,* as well as Pushkin's tales, Russian folk tales, and all kinds of other works of fantasy.

But it was too soon to celebrate total victory. I was convinced of this through a personal experience. I had had occasion to publish that same year, in the magazine *Iozh [Hedgehog],* the story of the ancient myth about Perseus, Andromeda, and Medusa the Gorgon. The editorial office of this periodical promptly received a letter fròm an educator in Gomel:

"Esteemed Comrade Editor! Having read in your magazine, *Iozh,* the Greek fairy tale that appeared on page 24 of issue number 1, 'Brave Perseus,' the children in my school surrounded me and asked why such nonsense is being published in our Soviet magazines. . . . How can we explain to children all the absurdity and thoughtlessness of the episodes described in this story, so full of the most nonsensical and foolish superstitions? In my opinion, this fairy tale lacks all artistic and literary beauty. . . ."

This letter was signed: "School Director, A. Rappoport."

I felt like pointing out humbly to Rappoport that this very myth about Perseus, precisely because of its beauty and artistic merit, had attracted, over the centuries, first-rate sculptors, playwrights, poets —Ovid, Sophocles, Euripides, Benvenuto Cellini, Corneille, Rubens, Titian, Heredia, and Canova.

I felt also like reminding him about Marx, who repeatedly stated that the ancient Greek epoch, with its ancient Greek art developed from mythology, "continues to offer us aesthetic pleasures and in a definite way safeguards the importance of quality and attainable standards." [11]

But the Rappoports ignore both Euripides and Marx. And they try to justify themselves by attributing objections to the children. From the way school director Rappoport put it, one would think that the children in his charge were extremely enraged when they saw "Perseus" in the magazine, and that they at once voiced a collective protest against the publishing of ancient Greek myths.

I hope he will forgive me if I say that I do not believe this. It is impossible that there were no normal youngsters in his entire school who had a lively poetic sensitivity! It is also impossible that he had succeeded in thoroughly atrophying in all his pupils their natural attraction to fantasy! And if there were two or three children who did not understand this legend, it was Rappoport's duty to explain it to them.

Using "Perseus" as a starting point for a discussion in a school assembly, he could have talked with the students about the origin of myths, about the constellations of Cassiopeia, Andromeda, Perseus; he could have delivered a lecture on the saturation of Christian religion with myths of pagan antiquity, about the connection between the mother of Perseus and the Virgin Mary, about the resemblance between the dragon who was going to devour Andromeda and the whale who swallowed the Biblical Jonah, and so on. All this, of course, he would have done if he had been an educated man. However, since he was ignorant, he incited the children against the most treasured works of art and bothered editors of children's magazines with absurd and ludicrous complaints.

The absurdity of such complaints is seen, in my opinion, in the claim that a genuinely poetic work published for Soviet children—be it a legend about Ilia Muramets or Reynard the Fox, or Munchausen, or Perseus—is politically harmful; by means of such demagogy these people justify their obscurantism.

They consider the myth or the fairy tale a threat to Leninism!

The privileged classes of all lands have until now deprived the toiling multitudes of the opportunity to learn about Euripides, Sophocles, and Ovid, about Benvenuto Cellini; but now, precisely because of Leninism, these masses have made available to themselves the colossal cultural treasures that were previously not within their reach.

If thousands and tens of thousands of workers in the Soviet Union now delight in Shakespeare, Mozart, and Rembrandt, if their children now fill the music conservatories and the art academies—all this is owing to the victory of Leninism.

He must be a hopeless Tartuffe who pretends that the least harm will be done to Leninism if we offer the Soviet child intelligently the myth of Prometheus, the poems about the flight of Icarus, the story about Odysseus, and the legend of Hercules.

I have deliberately quoted here Director Rappoport's letter because such as he are not unique even now. He has more than a few allies, and, although they no longer have the opportunity to display their narrow views in magazine and newspaper articles, they stubbornly follow the same theories in practicing their professions in the field of child education, and they keep from the young every work of art and genius if it is called a myth or a fairy tale. They thus reveal their shameless ignorance, which is usually equaled by their smug self-assurance.

I could understand it if my critic had taken objection to the interpretation I had given to the myth of Perseus. It would have been quite instructive to compare my version of it with those created for American and English children by Nathaniel Hawthorne and Charles Kingsley. But Rappoport was unable to undertake this task because it required thought and knowledge, and not merely the shaking of a fist.

I have given so much attention to Rappoport because these leftist educators still use quasi-revolutionary slogans to hinder and distort the literary development of Soviet children. They have quieted down in Moscow and in Leningrad, but in peripheral areas they still carry on as before. And every time the Children's Publishing Bureau or the Young Guard Publishing House puts out new editions of *Hiawatha,* or the tales of Pushkin or Munchausen, these enemies of childhood scream: "The Revolution is in danger"—and they save the Revolution from Pushkin. . . .

These "principled" opponents of the fairy tale use a typical method in their attacks—leftist slogans and the bravado of naked ignorance.

Narrow-minded Methods of Criticism (1956)

But the years passed, and all these obscurantists were overwhelmed by the forceful opposition of Soviet society. Articles began to appear more and more often extolling the great educational value of the fairy tale.

Now it is regarded as a generally recognized truth that the fairy tale develops, enriches, and humanizes the child's psyche, since the child who listens to fairy tales feels like an active participant and always identifies himself with those characters who crusade for justice, goodness, and freedom. It is in this active sympathy of little children with the high-minded and brave heroes of literary invention that lies the educational value of the literature of fantasy.

How can one help but be happy about the new generation of children! Finally they will be given, in abundant quantities, the nourishing, vitamin-filled, spiritual food that will ensure their normal and proper mental growth. It has been a long time since one encountered in print those "daredevils" who used to dare to come out openly against fairy tales and fantasy.

In our present way of life and in our present educational practice, the fairy tale no longer frightens anyone. Major and regional publishing establishments now provide children, unhindered, with Ukrainian, Azerbaidzhanian, Chinese, Hindu, Rumanian fairy tales, to say nothing of Danish, French, and German ones. The record of the writings about the general harm of fairy tales is now in archives —and forgotten. At present this question is considered in a much more circumspect way: Could specific fairy tales be harmful to children? Could a certain fairy tale inflict on them a grave trauma? This is a legitimate concern and one can only respect it.

But it is sad to think that our wide experience in education has not yet resulted in more firm principles for ascertaining the injury or the benefit of this or that kind of fairy tale. It is sad that this lack of verifiable theories opens up a wide field for narrow-minded or arbitrary judgments.

A case in point is my tale, *Mukha-Tsokotukha*. The well-known composer, M. I. Krasev, wrote an opera based on this tale. After attending this opera, an inhabitant of Zabaikal, Comrade Vladimir V——skii, wrote to the *Literaturnaia Gazeta* [*The Literary Gazette*]:

"Such tales do not deserve to be put to music or even to be brought into the world. This story evokes in children a definite sympathy for a poor, undeservedly suffering fly, for a 'brave' mosquito, and for other parasites. And this is very strange: on the one hand, in our country, we carry on a systematic, relentless war against insects, and, on the other hand, certain writers bring into the world works that strive to evoke sympathy for these parasites."

The *Literaturnaia Gazeta* refused to share his panic. He then took his complaint elsewhere, and his letter was forwarded to the Committee for Children's Literature of the Writers' Union. In this letter he repeated his attack on *Mukha* and, at the same time, included with it Charushin's fairy tale, *Volchishko* [*The Wolf Pup*], in which, to Comrade Vladimir V——skii's great indignation, little children are encouraged to feel a pernicious sympathy for wolves.

In my opinion, this man had the right to object. All that we writers produce, readers have a right to judge as they please, and to express their opinions in any way they please. And if these opinions are wrong, no one hampers any one of us from defending the truth and making a protest against the accusation.

I shall therefore attempt to take advantage of this privilege, especially since the views of the critic from Zabaikal impress me as being extremely typical of the majority of similar opinions. He represents legions of such thinkers who measure children's literary works with exactly the same yardstick.

This, of course, the Committee on Children's Literature of the Writers' Union could not fail to understand. I am certain that, first of all, it pointed out to the accuser of *Volchishko* and of *Mukha* the total inapplicability of utilitarian criteria in judging the harm or the usefulness of fairy tales. If one were to apply such criteria it would be necessary to reject and destroy not only these two innocent tales, but dozens of others, and, primarily, folk tales, folk songs, and lullabies about rabbits in which the most tender sentiments are expressed toward those gluttons and saboteurs. Rabbits, baby rabbits, darling little rabbits, pretty little rabbits—thus, from time immemorial, are they referred to in our folklore for children, and the very abundance of similar endearing forms proves that ordinary folk are, indeed, not bad educators! They are not in the least afraid to indoctrinate their little ones with a love for these gluttonous creatures:

> My white little rabbit,
> My gray little rabbit,
> Darling rabbit, dance a little,
> Darling rabbit, prance a little!

If we were to apply the utilitarian criteria suggested by the critic from Zabaikal, we would have to take away from children Nekrasov's *Grandfather Mazaii,* who stimulates in the hearts of little ones a warm compassion for rabbits:

> And rabbits too—move us to tears of pity!
>
> [*Zaitsy vot tozhe—ikh zhalko do slioz!*]

They move us to tears of pity—just think of it! These voracious despoilers of vegetable gardens move us to tears! And how happy are children, how they rejoice when Mazaii saves all these rabbits from perishing and lets them run off into the forest so that they may, horrors!—continue to multiply freely and in freedom.

According to E. A. Flerina, "the kindergarten teacher barely manages to finish reading this excerpt from *Grandfather Mazaii and the Rabbits* when the children say, with admiration, 'He's a good grandpa—a kind one; he saved all the rabbits.' " [12]

And, as if this were not enough to make the disaster complete, our folklore instills in children the idea that rabbits are true and devoted friends of man, guarding his vegetable gardens from plunderers, as if they themselves not only do not ruin cabbages but even water and take care of them:

> And I, the rabbit, the rabbit gray,
> Go about the garden every day,
> And guard the green cabbages
> From all kinds of ravagers,
> For the peasant, without muttering,
> I plant them and do the watering.[13]

It is clear then, if we were to take the position of the critic from Zabaikal, we would have to hide this song from little tots because it gives them a wrong idea about these "enemies of humanity." And, likewise, we would have to withdraw from circulation Leo Tolstoy's tale, *The Three Bears,* in which we find a similar folk sympathy for these undoers of country cows.

And what are we to do with the folk tale, *Finist, the Serene Falcon,* in which the gray wolf is presented to the small fry as a benefactor and friend of man, and with the folk tale, *The Enchanted Ring,* in which the little mouse appears as a benefactor and friend of man?

"Yes, I see now that I reacted hastily," Vladimir from Zabaikal might say with a sigh. "But, please be good enough to explain why the people and, following their example, a great folk poet forgot that the losses due to the destruction of vegetables and fruit trees by rabbits amount to millions of rubles? Why is it that the very same peasants who are vitally interested in the extermination of these marauders, instill in their children a lively compassion for them?"

"Of course, it is not difficult to explain this," the Committee of the Writers' Union should have answered. "The fact is that the people, through their long experience of a thousand years, have had the opportunity to become convinced that no matter how deeply the small children fall in love with little gray or white rabbits, little rabbits, darling little rabbits, these tots, when they become men, will participate with pleasure in the hunting of rabbits. No fairy tales heard or read in childhood would keep them then from pursuing rabbits without mercy. Creating their immortal children's songs and tales, the people understood very well that they were not meant to serve the purpose of forewarning little ones which creatures are harmful and which are useful. The child's fairy tale has other functions which are a thousand times more important than this classification of animals."

"What are these functions?" the pacified Vladimir V——skii might ask.

"These tasks are major ones," the Committee for Children's Literature should have answered. "And we might even say that they are formidable. But notice first of all that while fulfilling their important purpose, folk tales, or just the tales of great writers, treat with frank indifference the yardstick you have suggested for ascertaining their useful purpose. This was illustrated, for example, in the folk tale so dearly loved by children, *About the Gray Wolf and Prince Ivan*, where, in mockery of your theories, the wolf appears as a good soul, obtaining for his friend Ivan not only a gold-maned horse but a firebird and Elena the Fair, so that from the very beginning of this story children feel well disposed to the wolf.

"This was also expressed in a tale about another wolf, a tale written by Leo Tolstoy in which a wolf is depicted as freedom-loving and brave, refusing, for the sake of liberty, a life of plenty and security.

"And bears—every variety of 'Mishkas,' Bruins, 'Michael Potapiches'—need we say anything about how fascinating they were made for millions of children by the same folklore! And who does not know what the most treasured toys of small children are these same little bears [*mishkas*]—wooden ones, stuffed ones, velvet ones—designed specially so that children can stroke them, lull them to sleep, pity and caress them, wrap them in rags, feed them with imaginary *kasha*, protect them from imaginary misfortunes.

"And one has to be out of his mind and completely alienated from the realities of life, when seeing in some little Johnny's [*Vania's*] arms a velvet toy bear, to take it away from him, fearing that because of it, when he becomes a John [*Ivan*], he will not aim his gun or use his hunting pole at a live bear."

This, or approximately this, should have been the answer of the Committee on Children's Literature of the Writers' Union. But to my great astonishment, its answer was completely different:

"You are right in the way you pose your question," was its first remark. "Regrettably, some of our writers, who work in the field of fairy tales for preschool children, actually, for the sake of charming them, make mistakes, assigning to harmful animals, birds, and insects qualities of real heroes."

In the light of this approach to children's tales, such works as

these must be considered mistakes: the delightful folk tale by
Zhukovsky about the charitable wolf, in which the poet, following
the example of folklore, glorifies the humaneness of wolves; the
tale by Leo Tolstoy about the bear in the cart to whom children
respond with so much affection; and Pushkin's tale about Saltan
which arouses children's sympathy for a mosquito. Who among us
did not, in his childhood, clap his hands with delight when he heard
the famous lines by Pushkin:

> Czar Saltan at this wonder wondered,
> While the mosquito with anger thundered
> As it aimed at and straight did fly
> Into the cook's mean right eye.
> Pale she grew, was struck with fear,
> Tried to faint, and fell on her rear,
> As servants, in-laws, and her son, Kiril,
> The poor mosquito tried to kill.

Why, might one ask, did Pushkin, Zhukovsky, and Tolstoy commit
this strange "error"?

The Committee on Children's Literature answered this question
exactly as follows:

"This is explained, in our view," they wrote, "by inattention to
life's truths and an ignorance of nature in one's own land."

Establishing in this indirect way that Pushkin, Zhukovsky, Leo
Tolstoy, and, together with them, also Nekrasov, did not know
nature in their own country and that they were inattentive to life's
truths, the Committee on Children's Literature at the same time
declared, contrary to all evidence, that the Russian people in their
folklore chose to be silent about harmful animals—about the above-
mentioned rabbits, wolves, mice, and bears.

And for what reason did the committee make these denials of
the truth? In order to derive from them a practical deduction: the
radio opera by the composer Krasev, based on my tale, *Mukha-Tsokotukha*, was declared harmful and no longer resounds in the ether.

I repeat: the assumptions and the methods of our critic from
Zabaikal are extremely typical of many comparable expressions of
opinion. And, of course, I would not dwell so long on these opinions
if basically they did not harbor a confusion that has a world-view
scope.

As I have already indicated, the people, through their experience of a thousand years, have come to the unshakable conviction that those fairy-tale images that surround the child in his first years will not remain unchanged in his mind, and that in the process of his maturing and growing, under the influence of experience, they will undergo a thorough reëvaluation.

There are still many people today who are incapable of seeing the life of a child as a process, that is, as being in constant flux, change, and development. Such people are still under the illusion that a child is merely like a trunk, and that only what is put into it will be found there later. If love for a wolf or a mosquito or a fly is placed in a child's soul—it will remain there to the end of his days! And these people try to cram into this "trunk" as many good things as possible, and are very surprised when they later find in it not all the things they stored there.

These men and women forget that, just as the egg does not resemble the chick and the seed does not resemble the tree, a three-year-old child does not resemble the man that he will subsequently become. A child is only a rough draft of a man, and much will be deleted from this rough draft and much will be added to it before a Michurin * or a Tsiolkovsky † emerges from a big-eyed, rosy-cheeked, and ticklish Yurik—or a man of very base metal. Because a three-year-old child goes through a period when he likes to break toys, it does not follow that by the time he is fifteen he will have become a specialist in cracking fireproof safes.

This is the way those educators and parents think who do not take into account the dialectic development of the human being. They think as the pregnant woman who, weeping bitterly when she found out that at two or three months the embryo in her womb had developed gills and a tail, said:

"I don't want my little Vania to have a tail!"

Meanwhile both the gills and the tail will disappear before he is born.

---

* Ivan Michurin (1855–1935) was a celebrated Russian-Soviet botanist, agronomist, naturalist, and evolutionist.

† Konstantin Tsiolkovsky (1857–1935) was a Russian-Soviet scientist in aerodynamics, rocketry, and interplanetary research.

These dull people imagine that every fairy tale told to a youngster will remain with him his entire life, with its morals and fantasy, and will condition his entire existence. This was the naïve conviction that served as the basis for the suppression of fairy tales in the time of the pedologists.

In Rostov-on-Don, some fellow whose name began with a "P" (Peredonov, perhaps?) published an article at that time in which he fiercely criticized the famous tale about Tom Thumb because there were cannibals in it. Obviously he assumed that the child who read this tale would grow up to be a cannibal.

"Why do you nourish yourself on human flesh?" he would be asked by his horrified neighbors.

"When I was a child someone read to me *Tom Thumb.*"

And in the town of Chkalov, a certain Bulgakov actually printed, on real paper, that the fairy tale is a school for scandal and debauchery because, for instance, in the story of Cinderella, the mean stepmother, because of her urge to torture someone, throws cinders into her stepdaughter's lentil soup and is therefore undoubtedly a sadist; and the prince, moved to rapture by the glass slipper of poor Cinderella [*Zolushka*], is a disguised fetishist of women's small feet!

In the city of Gorki a woman wrote a short article about the child who listens to many fairy tales and will therefore become indoctrinated with an attitude of moral indifference. He will begin to seek not collective but individual happiness, evidently becoming an embezzler or a fence for stolen goods.

Placing him behind bars, the judge will no doubt say to him:

"If only you had not read in your childhood *Puss in Boots!!*"

The persecutors of the fairy tale counted on the opinions of ignorant people like these, who believed that there were no ideas in fairy tales which would not remain in the child's mind to condition him for the next twenty or thirty years, and that these ideas did not undergo any metamorphosis. They believed that when a five-year-old, to whom was read, for instance, the fairy tale about the magic carpet, reached the age of thirty he would not even want to hear of Dneprostrois and would remain, to the end of his days, a dreamer, a romantic, a mystic.

This is obscurantist medieval thinking which assumes that the conceptions, thoughts, and reactions of children become congealed forever after.

However, the objects of the child's affection will change more than once with the passing of time. Therefore, storytellers do not worry unduly about the proper selection of these objects and their beneficial or harmful relation to mankind. The goal of storytellers is quite different. It consists of fostering in the child, at whatever cost, compassion and humaneness—this miraculous ability of man to be disturbed by another being's misfortunes, to feel joy about another being's happiness, to experience another's fate as one's own. Storytellers take trouble to teach the child in his early years to participate with concern in the lives of imaginary people and animals, and to make sure that in this way he will escape the narrow frame of his egocentric interests and feelings.

Because it is natural for a child to be on the side of the kind, the courageous, and the unjustly offended when listening to a fairy tale, whether it is Prince Ivan or Peter Rabbit or the Fearless Spider, our only goal is to awaken, nurture, and strengthen in the responsive soul of the child this invaluable ability to feel compassion for another's unhappiness and to share in another's happiness—without this a man is inhuman. Only this ability, inherent in the individual from early childhood and developed to a high degree in the course of maturing, has begotten and will beget in the future the Bestuzhevs, the Pirogovs, the Nekrasovs, the Chekhovs, the Gorkis.

All that has been recounted in this chapter occurred three or four years ago. At present there is a new spirit in the Committee on Children's Literature of the Writers' Union. But does this mean that there no longer exist "guardians" of the national welfare who are ready to take from children this or that work of art, justifying themselves by their regressive dogmas?

The misfortune is that these dogmas are still terribly alive. In the first place, they still impress naïve minds with their false logic. Second, those who apply these dogmas in a controversy over this or that children's book simultaneously credit themselves with the noble role of a passionate defender of the social good. It is quite tempting to take on this role—especially for the Tartuffes and the bureaucrats. It is therefore not so easy to eradicate from our point of view this kind of criticism, and it would be nonsensical to anticipate a speedy and total victory. There will be relapses—and not just once more. It will be a stubborn battle. And I will be sincerely happy if I have succeeded here, even partially, even to an insignificant degree, in exposing this pernicious method of criticism which is so utterly wrong in judging the most important question of the educational value of any children's book.

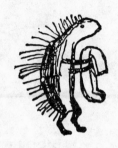

CHAPTER VI

Conversation with Beginners

"COMMANDMENTS" FOR
CHILDREN'S POETS

We Learn from Folklore and from Children

A wonderful thing happened in Russia to a certain young man. He had come to the capital to study; surprising himself, and without much effort, he created a book of genius, a lasting addition to Russian literature which has survived more than a hundred years and, without doubt, will survive another century.

The nineteen-year-old round-cheeked, beardless youth who had just left the provincial school bench—how surprised he would have been had someone predicted then, in 1834, the great destiny of his near-juvenile endeavor!

And how loudly would the critics of that day have laughed if anyone had voiced the opinion that the humble manuscript of this awkward provincial youth was a classical work of Russian poetry, which would still excite millions of hearts when many books by other writers—books by writers whom they were proclaiming as great—would lie forgotten under layers of eternal library dust, although these writers were the idols of the reading public.

The name of this youth was Peter Ershov; his great book was *The Little Humpbacked-Horse* [*Konek-gorbunok*].

There were two strange developments in the literary biography of Ershov. First, why, after writing his famous book when still a youth, did he never again write anything that approximated the outstanding literary quality of his early masterpiece? He lived long and he had enough time to produce at least ten such delightful books, but in *The Little Humpbacked-Horse* he seemed to have spent his entire giftedness. He did not abandon writing but continued to write, at times pretentiously, but almost invariably his works were superficial and devoid of anything vivid or original. Soon after finishing *The Little Humpbacked-Horse* he wrote a turgid poem in the form of a mystic ballad, then a libretto for an opera,[1] and so on. All this was not bad writing, but it was in no way comparable to the greatness of his one masterpiece.

The second development in Ershov's literary career seems to me to have been even stranger than the first. Why, after bringing forth this children's book, which has become a staple for all five-, six-, and seven-year-old Russian youngsters, did Ershov never suspect that he had written a children's book? Nor did anyone else around him suspect this. Bibliographies listed the work as a book for adult readers. Critics estimated its merits according to criteria used for adult books. Had Ershov tried to place his book in a magazine for the young, his *Little Humpbacked-Horse* would have been kicked out as a village peasant [*muzhik*] trying to crash a governor's ball.

Throughout his long life Ershov never again returned to the simple style of his masterpiece—to the peasant vernacular—but strived to cultivate the high-flown poetic style of his times. This, I believe, explains the first strange development in his writing career. A master of the Russian folk idiom, he rejected this idiom over which he had complete command, scorned it, and never again made any attempt to return to it in his creative work after writing the *Humpbacked-Horse*.

This was the cause of the weakening of his talent and of his ultimate failure as a writer. He tore himself away from the roots that
nourished his genius—from the colloquial speech of the common
people, from folk humor, from the common people's view of life,
and from their aesthetics. This, it seems to me, is the key, as well, to
the second unusual aspect of his tragic story.

During the reign of Nicholas I,* *The Little Humpbacked-Horse*
was suppressed by the censors for a long time. Then, from time to
time, it was printed as a popular book for readers of low caliber,
and it enjoyed a brisk sale at market places where it was peddled in
the same way as cotton yard goods, booklets interpreting dreams,
icons, and pastry. After thirty years this great work finally became
part of Russian literature, but as a book for children. They "wrested"
it from the adults and took possession of it forever as a precious
prize; it was only then that grownups realized that this work was, indeed, good nourishment for the young—tasty, wholesome, hunger-
satisfying, contributing to their spiritual growth.

By that time tremendous social changes began to take place in
our country. Russian education began to serve the common man
who could not but respond to the democratic idea and the popular
idiom of Ershov's "plebeian" epic poem.

Having appropriated this book as their own, children bequeathed
it to their grandchildren, their great-grandchildren, and their great-
great-grandchildren, and it has become impossible to imagine a generation of Russian children who could get along without Ershov's
book.

This was a great lesson for all of us. In the symbolic fate of *The
Little Humpbacked-Horse* was reflected the affinity between children
and the common people. That which pertained to children and to
ordinary folk emerged as synonymous.

Similar incidents in the history of our literature are not rare.
Many books originally written for adults subsequently became children's books on the strength of their folk idiom. The fate of Ershov's
book was similar to that of Pushkin's tales. Pushkin had written
them for adults as assimilations and adaptations of folklore. They

---

* Nicholas I reigned from 1825 to 1855.

were received with arrogant aversion and, it was claimed, they demonstrated a deterioration of Pushkin's talent. Critics were angry, asking how Pushkin dared spend any of his creative power on so "debased" a genre. And the children, whom the poet had not intended to address in such tales as *Saltan*, *The Golden Cockerel*, *Czar's Daughter*, accepted them into their spiritual domain and thus demonstrated once more that folk poetry, in its highest attainments, is often poetry for children.

All Pushkin's tales—every one of them—were peasant tales with peasant vernacular and diction.

And if we recall that the fables of Krylov * also appeared as writings for adults, and that they also resurrected popular speech with unequaled perfection, we shall have the full right to say that the great Russian people (that is, the Russian peasant, for the Russian population at that time was almost entirely rural) "dictated" to the gifted authors all the best children's books. From their lips the Russian people spoke and affirmed their faith in the eternal victory of kindness, mercy, and truth over the soul-thwarting cruelty of lies. Such were the poems of Nekrasov, the children's books by Leo Tolstoy, by Ushinsky—all saturated through and through with our folklore.

Parallel with these folklore-inspired books, another kind of nineteenth-century children's literature made its appearance, and the same thing happened to this literature as happened to Ershov's writings for adults. It alienated itself from the aesthetics, the humor, the ideals, and the tastes of the common people, and was therefore sterile.

The stormy renaissance which has created a "great literature for small children," and which started here, in the Soviet Union, about thirty years ago, reflects the deep inspiration that folklore has provided for Soviet culture. There is an abundance of examples proving how children's books have been enriched by it. It was noted long ago in the criticism of this literature that the poems for the young by Mayakovsky, for instance, "have a wealth of reminiscences from folklore," and that the beginning of his *The Tale of Petia the Fat*

---

* Ivan Krylov (1769–1844) was the most celebrated Russian writer of fables.

Child and Sima Who Was Thin is a typical folk numbers-rhyme
[*shchitalka*]: [2]

> There lived once
> Sima and Petey.
>
> Sima and Petey
> Were kiddies.
>
> Petey was 4
> And Sima was 7—
>
> And both together
> They were 11.

Discussing poetry, S. Marshak calls the attention of young writers
to the folk sources of much creative writing. And, of course, he
would not have been able to reproduce in his translations the spirit
of English folk rhymes if he had not been so attuned to the rhythm
and the style of Russian children's folklore. Agnia Barto also speaks
about the organic link between our poetry for the young and folk
poetry: "There is no doubt that verse for children has its laws of ex-
cellence. It makes special uses of the expressiveness of folk poetry. In
the best poems for children we find the hyperbole, the reiteration, the
alliteration, and an ingenious play on words, as well as the riddle
and the numbers-rhyme." [3]

I became aware of the great vigor of our folk literary tradition
through my own limited experience. When I started to compose
verse for the very young child, I could not find, for a long time, a
vital, intrinsically suitable style. Slowly, after many failures and
doubtful successes, I became convinced that the only "compass" on
this road for all children's poets—strong ones and weak ones—was
folk poetry (see, for example, my *Mukha-Tsokotukha, The Stolen
Sun, Fedorina's Misfortune*, etc.).

This does not mean, however, that our problem is how to imitate
slavishly ancient folklore. Carbon copies of folklore we can do without. Just the same, we cannot ignore the fact that the simple folk
had, over the centuries, developed in their songs, folk tales, fairy
tales, epic legends, and poetry, ideal aesthetic and didactic methods
of approach to the child's psyche; we would be quite wasteful if we
did not apply this experience of a thousand years and more.

But allow me to repeat that we must learn not only from the people; our second teacher is the child. At least I would never have dared to start writing my *Moidodyr* if I had not tried beforehand to ascertain the needs and the tastes of my young "readers," and if I had not sought the means of making my verse have the best effect on them. It must not be inferred from this that I was trying too hard to amuse and please the child. None of us may overlook the duty to educate him, to influence him, to shape his personality; we can succeed in this only if we make a full study of his mental processes and if we attempt to determine what poetic style would be most effective.

In those days, long ago, when I was still looking for the criteria of good writing for children, I finally formulated for myself a set of rules, which I called "commandments" [*zapovedi*], and I followed them when composing verse for children. Since these rules were, in a sense, suggested by the children themselves, I considered them largely immutable and believed them to be important for every poet trying to write for children. Neither S. Marshak, nor Mikhalkov, nor Barto, nor any other of my comrades in the literary service to children, had yet, at that time, begun their creative writing for the young. I was therefore unable to verify through their literary practices my own criteria or "commandments." I can say now, however, without any fear of being wrong, that, although the creative efforts of these remarkable poets suggested some changes in my rules, basically they and their work confirmed the correctness of my conclusions and criteria so far as poetry for the child "from two to five" was concerned.

Imagery and Action

My *first "commandment"* for children's poets has already been implied elsewhere in this book: their poems must be *graphic,* that is, every stanza, and at times every couplet, must suggest an illustration to the artist, since children think in terms of images. Those lines that serve no purpose for the illustrator are also largely useless to the child. The children's author must, so to speak, think in pictures. (If the reader leafs through my children's tales, he will find that *Tarakanishche* [*The Cockroach*] calls for twenty-eight illustrations accord-

ing to the number of images given; *Moidodyr* [*The Washstand*] calls
for twenty-three, etc.)

Poems printed without illustrations lose almost half of their ef-
fectiveness. "Mother, show me!" cried the child to whom one of our
editorial assistants read *Tarakanishche* from galleys, without the
illustrations. He felt that the pictures and the words were an integral
part of a whole. Because the child's vision initially absorbs not so
much the quality of objects as their movement, their action, the
subject matter of poetry for the very young must be so full of imagery,
so full of movement and change, that every few lines require a new
illustration. Where this is not true, children's verses, we might say,
do not work.

If you write a full page of poetry and find that it suggests only one
picture, consider this page useless. The rapid change of images is
our *second "commandment"* for young poets.

The *third rule* is that this verbal "painting" must be "lyrical" at
the same time; the poet-artist must be a poet-singer as well. It is not
enough for the child to see this or that episodic development expressed in verse and pictures. He needs to be able to sing and clap;
that is, he needs to be able to react to the verses as if they were his
own rhymed syllables [*ekiki*].* If the child can neither sing nor clap,
if the verses do not have the essence and the beat of their own nonsense rhymes, they will never move the hearts of these little ones. It
is small wonder, then, that the children's folklore from all lands,
which lends itself to singing and clapping, has survived and has remained intact over the centuries.

This "commandment" is harder "to obey" than any other—the
poet-artist is seldom also a poet-singer. These seem to be two an-
tagonistic categories of talent and mutually exclusive. Can we really
expect that every incident presented in the poem with graphic sensitivity must also, at the same time, affect the listener like a rhythmic
song that would stimulate him to happy clapping? I became fully
aware of the difficulty of this problem when I undertook the writing
of my first "poem for little ones." But I was convinced that the problem was basic and that without solving it one could not undertake

---

* Chukovsky coined the word *ekiki* to designate the nonsense rhymes that very
young children make up as they hop, skip, jump, and clap to them.

[This illustration appears in all the editions of Chukovsky's verse tale, *Moidodyr*. The word *"Moidodyr"* was created by the author to stand for an animated washstand moralizing about little boys and cleanliness.]

this work. It was essential to find a unique, lyric-epic style, suitable for narration and recitation and, at the same time, free from the typical diction of narration and recitation. It seemed to me that all types of narrative poems, and, in general, all long fables in verse, can react on small children only through a series of lyrical stanzas—each one having its own rhythm and its own emotional coloration. In developing the proper style for *The Crocodile* (1916), I tried in every way to vary the structure according to the emotions that the lines expressed—I changed from the trochee to the dactyl, from the couplet to the six-line stanza. This moving and changing of rhythm was for me the *fourth "commandment."*

Music

The *fifth "commandment"* for children's poets is to achieve a heightened musicality of poetic expression. It is remarkable that children's rhymed syllables [*ekiki*] are always melodic. Their musicality is achieved primarily by an unusual flow and fluidity of sound. Children would never permit in their own verses, impromptu or otherwise, the consonant clusters that often disfigure our "adult" poems for children. Nor did I ever find in a single rhyme composed by children such harsh, unpronounceable combinations of sounds as those that one finds in some published poems. Here is a typical line from a poem for children:

>   *Vdrug vzgrustnulos'* . . . [Suddenly sadness descended . . .]

This barbaric *v d r u g   v z g r* is beyond the strength of a child's larynx. This line was written by a certain Leningrad author; and it is equally painful to read the clumsy line composed by a Moscow poetess:

>   *Akh, pochashche b s shokoladom* . . .
>   [Oh! oftener with chocolate . . .]

One must despise children to offer them such tongue-breaking brick-bats! It would do no harm for the creators of similar verse to learn from the children whose throats they strain with such freakish sounds. One need only compare these two lines of verse: one composed by a child—*"Polovina utiuga"* ["half an iron"], and the other written by a grownup—"*Akh, pochashche b s shokoladom,*" to see the tremendous superiority of the three-year-old. In *polovina utiuga* only six consonants were needed for seven vowels, but in the line about the chocolate a full dozen consonants were needed for eight vowels.

Just listen to this melodic little "song" which Vitia Rammo sang to herself as she danced to it (Vitia was not yet two):

> Kossi minie, kossi koi,
> Lieba kussi, lieba koi
>
> Kossi baba, kossi koi,
> Kussi paki, kussi moi.
>
> Ioka kuku, shubka koi
> Lieba kusia, shubka koi.

These, of course, are meaningless rhymed syllables [*ekiki*]. Vitia could speak quite well, fully pronouncing all kinds of sound combinations but, when it came to rhymes, she preferred to arrange her consonants so that they would meet one another as seldom as possible. Except for the word "*shubka,*" the rest of the words are "designed" in such a way as to provide a vowel between every two consonants.

Remarkable was the means taken by two-year-old Alena Polezhaeva to avoid the clustering of consonants. Her mother informed me that when two consonants occurred contiguously, Alenushka would insert a vowel between them: thus, *ptichka* [little bird] became *patichka*, *kto* [who] became *kito*, *gde* [where] became *ghide*.

When writing children's verse, I tried, to the best of my ability, to attend to this clearly indicated preference and need of little children.

Rhymes—Poetic Style

The *sixth rule* has been discussed in detail in an earlier chapter. It is sufficient to say here that it calls for frequent rhyming—at least at the end of every few words. It is much more difficult for the young child to get the sense of the poem when rhyming is not contiguous.

The *seventh "commandment"* is that the words used for rhyming should be the main carriers of the meaning of the phrase in which they appear. They should carry the semantic load. Because the words that rhyme particularly attract the attention of the listening child, it is these words that must carry the greater part of the meaning. I consider this rule one of the most important, and try not to ignore it under any circumstances. I often experiment with my own and other writers' poems—I cover the left side of the page and try to tell the contents of the poem from the rhyming words on the right side. If I do not succeed in this, the poem is in for a revision, since it is not yet capable of reaching the young child.

The *eighth rule* is that every line of a poem must have a life of its own—it must be a syntactic whole because the child's thinking pulsates in the same rhythm as the verse. Each line in their own *ekiki* is an independent "sentence," and the number of lines equals the number of "sentences."

Older children use sentences expressed in two lines, as in

> We go with Chukosha in two's
> To buy for all new snowshoes.
>
> We'll buy, we'll buy snowshoes
> For ourselves and for Chukosh. . . .

[The children call Mr. Chukovsky "Chukosha" as an expression of familiarity and affection.]

But for the younger child long poems are usually written in couplets. Pushkin's *Saltan* and Ershov's *The Little Humpbacked-Horse* are, in reality, a chain of couplets. Here are a few typical lines from Pushkin's fairy tale of *Saltan:*

> The stars shine in the dark blue sky,
> The waves lash out in the dark blue sea.
>
> In the sky the cloud moves,
> In the sea the barrel is tossing.
>
> The Queen imprisoned in it struggles
> —A most unhappy widow.

"Oh! wave, my wave,
You're gay and free!

"You splash about at will,
Grinding down the rocks of the sea.

"You drown the shores of the earth,
You lift the ships in the sea.

"Do not ruin my life, oh, wave—
Lash out and carry me to land!"

After each couplet—a pause; every couplet is a separate and independent phrase. Children's verses do not permit any internal pauses, that is, the interruption of the melodic flow. Only in one of the poems composed by children did I find a carrying over to the next line and a slight one at that—only one instance of continuing the sentence outside the limits of the couplet:

The tiny sparrow hopped,
And on his way he swallowed
Crumbs of bread, that for him
I put on the window sill.

These lines were composed by Vanya F., four and a half years old.

Young Children Reject Adjectives

We have said above that children's vision most often observes not the quality but the movement of objects. From here stems our *ninth "commandment"* for children's writers: not to crowd their poems with adjectives. Poems enriched by epithets are not for small children; one never finds adjectives in verses made up by preschoolers. This is understandable because the epithet comes as a result of a longer acquaintance with the object. It is the fruit of experience and exploration not yet congruous with the preschooler's age.

The writers of children's poetry often forget this and overburden their verses with an enormous number of adjectives. For the young child this results in nothing but boredom, because what excites him in his literature is action and the quick succession of events. Since this is so, let us have more verbs and fewer adjectives! I consider the ratio of verbs to adjectives the best objective criterion of the suitability of a given poem for the child "from two to five."

It is the conviction of Stern * that in the developing vocabulary of the child nouns predominate at first, then verbs are added, and last—adjectives. He made the following observations with regard to a little girl's speech: when she was one year and three months old her entire vocabulary consisted of nouns; within the next five months they constituted only 78 per cent of her vocabulary, and verbs the remaining 22 per cent; three months after that nouns were only 63 per cent, verbs 23 per cent, and other parts of speech (including adjectives) 14 per cent. This ratio sins against a formal approach to grammar, but the general tendency of the linguistic development of children certainly is correctly reflected in it.

A love of adjectives is noticeable (and even then only to a limited degree) mainly in bookish, reflective children—a child who has an activist attitude to life builds almost all his speech on verbs. This is why I filled my tale, *Moidodyr,* from top to bottom, with verbs, and declared at the same time a merciless boycott of adjectives; I also assigned to every object maximum activity:

The quilt	[*Odealo*
Ran away!	*Ubezhalo!*
Away flew the sheet!	*Uletela prostynia!*
And the pillow,	*I podushka,*
Like a frog	*Kak liagushka*
Leaped from me	*Uskakala*
Down the street!	*Ot menia!*]

Of course, everything said in this chapter concerns only the preschool child. When children grow older nothing contributes so much

---

* William Stern (1851–1938) was a German psychologist and philosopher; much of his work concerned the linguistic and psychological development of young children.

to the maturing of their minds as the ever-increasing number of adjectives that enrich their perceptions and expressions.

The *tenth "commandment"* is that the predominant rhythm in young children's poetry must be that of the trochee (a long syllable followed by a short one, or an accented syllable followed by an unaccented one). A great deal has been said about this in chapter iii.

Poems for Play and Games

The *eleventh "commandment"* for children's poets is that children's verses must be suitable for play and games because, in reality, the activity of young and "middle-aged" preschoolers, with minor exceptions, takes the form of play. Most rhymed folk tales generate play and games. In my book, *The Telephone*, I tried in every way to give the children material for their favorite games of telephone. I should say that he who has no talent for playing with children had better not undertake the writing of children's poetry.

But children do not limit themselves to playing with objects— they also enjoy playing with sounds and words. This playing with sounds and words is extremely useful and is plentiful in children's folklore throughout the world. Even when the child grows older, he often has the need to comfort himself with word play, since he does not all at once get used to the fact that words fulfill mainly the businesslike function of communication. We all remember our word games [*poteshki*] originating among ourselves, when we were school children: "Steve stole Stephanie's string," "Clement cleaned Clara's clarinet," and so forth.

The preschooler is even more in need of such toying with words, and he gets an even greater delight from it. This also indicates that he is already quite sure of the correct usage of the words he distorts for his amusement. How the children laugh when I read to them my "*Cat*ousie and *Mou*sie," based on the distortion of words borrowed from the English folk tale:

> There once lived a mouse called Mousie,
> She suddenly saw a cat called Catousie.

The Last "Commandments"

We see from all this that children's poetry should be written in a special way, differently from the way poetry would be written for adults, and that it must be evaluated according to special criteria. But it does not follow from this that the children's poet has the right to ignore the standards that one applies to poetry for adults. Children's poetry, in addition to satisfying the special requirements just discussed, must have the skill, the virtuosity, the technical soundness of poetry for adults. A bad poem could never be good for children. This, in summary, is the *twelfth "commandment."*

There is also a *thirteenth* one. We, children's poets, must not only adapt our writing to the needs of the young—we must also, through our creations, bring the children within reach of our adult perceptions and thoughts. Of course, we should proceed slowly and with utmost caution, without straining the child's readiness and the child's nature. However, if we fail to help the child [to reach out for new perceptions and thoughts], we must resign from our role as his educators. It follows, therefore, that [as we extend our writing to older children] we deliberately, if gradually, abandon all the "commandments" necessary for the best verse writing for the very young, so as to develop in the growing child an ever-maturing and strongly instilled understanding, appreciation, and love of the great poets. This will be a prolonged educational process in the art of poetry for which, for some reason, we do not yet show sufficient concern. The approach to the education in poetry of the older preschooler should, therefore, begin with the adoption of more advanced stylistic standards which will gradually set aside the "commandments" we formulated, all of them, that is, except one—the twelfth—which insists on excellent poetic quality in poetry for beginners. This rule must not be violated under any circumstances.

Unfortunately, many educators, book reviewers, and literary critics still judge children's verses exclusively on the basis of content, unaware that the most valuable content will be hopelessly compromised if expressed in careless and inferior poetic form—so that, for the sake of the content itself, one must first of all make a study of the stylistic demands of children's poetry.

We have spoken in this chapter in terms of "commandments," a rather presumptuous word for these flexible rules. These "commandments" are merely guideposts built for himself by a beginning children's poet who strived to come closer to the mind of small children so as to be most effective in his communication with them.

The Cockroach

by Kornei Chukovsky

[Kornei Chukovsky's carefully developed theories about how children's poets should write for the very young, so impressively expressed in the last chapter of this book, are fully demonstrated in the poem, *The Cockroach (Tarakanishche)*, one of his best-known animal tales, first published in 1924. Like all his tales in verse, it is chock-full of imagery, action, rhythm, and rollicking rhymes, and leaves the child with something to think about.

The Cockroach

PART ONE

Here comes a pike
Riding a bike.

Followed by a cat—all black—
On a scooter front-to-back.

Next, five mosquitoes come into sight,
Flying along on a yellow kite.

Then arrives Mousie Mollie
On a limping, smiling collie.

And a stork astride a mare,
And a bear in a wheel-chair.

Little rabbits, soft and huggy,
Come riding in a baby buggy.

A frog does a funny trick,
Diving down from a broomstick.

Camels, horses, and donkeys
Come carrying monkeys.

A white unicorn
Trots, blowing a horn.

Slowly along the road
Hasten a turtle and a toad.

"Be careful! Don't crush the ants,"
A hippo warns the elephants.

To the picnic they all come,
Munching candy and cake,

In a very merry mood,
For a day at the lake.

Then suddenly they grow numb and still!
Who's that coming round that hill?!

A fierce and dreadful Roach!
A mean cock-cock-*Cockroach!*

"Don't you dare to approach!"
He roars, he rages:

"I'll lock you in cages!
And swallow you ALL
Like one tiny meatball!

"Or with a twitch of my mustache,
I'll turn you all to succotash!"

The birds—they shudder!
The beasts—they flutter!

The poor crocodile
Forgets how to smile!

The hungry wolves, in their alarm,
Though meaning no evil or harm,
Right then and there they sup,
Gobbling one another up!

And a terrified lady dog.
Falls into a faint
On a prickly hedgehog!

Alas! Not one dares to fight,
Every bird and beast takes flight!

The Lobster, backing up a mile,
Murmurs with a bitter smile:

"I, too, have a long mustache,
I, too, can make succotash . . ."

The Cockroach continues to roar,
The Lobster backs up some more.

Now the Lion climbs a hill;
From there he speaks his royal will:

"We must regain our happy land!
Against the brute we'll take a stand!

"And to the warrior who fears not this
   foe,
Who this monster will overthrow,
To him I'll give a juicy bone
And the finest pine cone!

The creatures in one eager crowd,
Surge forth and cry out loud:

"We do not fear this nasty foe,
With tooth and claw
We'll lay him low!"

And they all rush to do battle—
Birds, fish, fowl, and cattle.

But the Roach moves his mustache
And bellows: "SUCCOTASH!"

One and all they beat a retreat.
The enemy they don't defeat!

Into the fields and woods they dash—
Terrorized by the Roach's mustache!

The lion shouts: "What a disgrace!
Come back! Come out and show your
    face!
Pin the enemy with your horns—
Bulls, rhinocceros, unicorns!"

But each in his hiding place stays,
And wails:"Horns aren't cheap these
    days . . . .
And our skin is precious too—
What you ask of us, we cannot do!"

Caught in nettles the crocodiles twitch,
And the elephants get stuck in a ditch.

Lo! All that's heard now
Is the flow of their tears;
All that's seen now
Is the trembling of their ears!

And the shark, scared and pale,
With a flail of his tail,
Slithers into the lake—
Not like a shark, like a snake!

While the cunning little skunk
Already packs his trunk.

PART TWO

To the Cockroach they all yield—
He's now lord o'er wood and field.
He struts about among them,
Rubbing his big tummy,
Looks at their young ones
And thinks: "How very yummy!"

Gazes at the little ones with greed,
Orders supper to be brought him with
    speed!

"I want no beans or corn,
But flesh of baby unicorn;
Other youngsters as well—
Those with a savory smell."

The poor, poor parents
Are in distress.
Their dear babes
They hug and caress:

For what mother could give up her child,
Her baby tame or her baby wild?!
So that the monster could devour
Her precious crumb, her little flower!

So mommies and daddies moan and cry
As they bid their infants good-bye!

And the monster is secretly cursed:
"May the glutton blow up!
May he burst!"

But now we see another picture:
The Kangaroo, that nimble creature—
Leaps, leaps—she's at the Roach's hill,
And for a moment all are mute
As she points to the mustached brute:

"A monster?! Where?!
A Giant?! There?!

"It's a roach, a roach, a wee-bit roach,
A wee-little beetle you fear to approach.
Look! It's a midge, a mite,
A bug that can't even bite!

"For our trouble *we're* to blame!
What a shame!
What a shame!"

The Hippo then comes forth
With slow pace and worried face,
Muttering in an anxious way:

"Please go away, go away!
Your words will make him very mad,
He may think of something very bad!
Go, Kangaroo, Kangaroo,
Go, go back to your zoo!"

Then the Hippo falls still,
Surprised by a sudden trill . . .
"Cheek-chee-reek, cheeky-reeky,
Cheek-chee-reek."
And from behind a bush
They see it peek.

Hop-hop-hop—comes the reckless
fellow,
A gay and carefree little Sparrow.
And right there, on the Roach's hill,
With his cheeky-reeky trill,
Peck, peck, peck—
NO MORE ROACH!
Not a smidgen, not a speck!

He's swallowed in a flash,
All of him and his mustache!

PART THREE

What joy! What glee!
All the creatures again are free!

The Sparrow is praised and
On loving paws it's raised—
There's a parade,
A celebration,
A masquerade!

The mules bray a song,
Hippo strikes his gong.

To honor the Sparrow, a path is cleared:
The goat sweeps it with his beard.

The sheepish sheep
Don't sing but hum,
The bold baboon
Beats a drum.

And from the roof the joyous bats,
Wave their hankies and their hats.

But when the elephants start to prance,
To clap and stomp a happy dance,
The orange moon shakes loose—
And falls right on big Moose!

Like a pinwheel it falls from the sky,
Now all is dark—save the firefly!

WHAT TO DO?!
The Monkeys who are no fools,
With hammers, nails, and other tools,

In a row make a trek,
Up the Giraffe's long, long neck.

To the sky the moon is nailed,
The Monkeys bow as they're hailed.

Again the moon sheds its light,
Again the world is friendly, bright.

[An illustration for the final "scene" which appears in all the Russian editions of *Tarakanishche* (*The Cockroach*).]

Notes

Chapter I. A Linguistic Genius

1. Lev N. Tolstoy, *Polnoe sobranie sochinenii* [*Complete Collected Works*] (Jubilee ed.; Moscow, 1936), VIII, 70.

2. A. N. Gvozdev, *Formirovanie u rebionka grammaticheskovo stroia russkovo iazyka* [*The Mastering by the Child of the Grammatical Structures of the Russian Language*] (Moscow, 1949), Part I, pp. 231, 252.

3. These figures were obtained from an article by A. P. Semenova, "Psikhologicheskii analiz ponimania allegorii, metafor i sravnenia" ["A Psychological Analysis of Children's Understanding of Allegories, Metaphors, and Similes], *Uchionye zapiski Leningradskovo pedagogicheskovo instituta imeni A. I. Gerzena*, XXXV (1941), 180.

4. Lev N. Tolstoy, *Sobranie khudozhestvennykh proizvedenii* [*Collected Literary Works*], Izd. Pravda (*Ogonëk*) (1948), p. 247.

5. See, for instance, articles by L. A. Pen'evskaia, "Rasskazyvanie kak sredstvo obucheniia sviaznoi rechi" ["Narrating as a Means of Training Children to Speak Coherently"], *Izvestiia Akademii pedagogicheskikh nauk*, no. 16 (1948); by T. E. Tikhomirova, "Rabota nad grammaticheskoi pravil'nostiu rechi detei" ["Training Children in Correct Grammatical Usage"], *Doshkol'noe vospitanie*, no. 1 (1953); by A. S. Murav'eva, "Vospitanie pravil'noi rechi u detei mladshei grupy" ["Teaching Correct Speech to Young Preschoolers"], *Doshkol'noe vospitanie*, no. 4 (1953); by E. V. Aristoteleva, "Obuchenie detei rodnomu iazyku" ["Teaching Children Their Native Language"], *Doshkol'noe vospitanie*, no. 8 (1953).

Chapter II. The Tireless Explorer

1. I have used this example found in the article by A. V. Zaporozhets, "Razvitie logicheskovo myshlenia u detei v doshkol'nom vozraste" ["The Development of Logical Thinking in Preschool Children"], in *Voprosy psikhologii rebionka* (Moscow-Leningrad, 1948), p. 82.

2. E. I. Zalkind, "Kak otvechat' na voprosy detei" ["How To Answer Children's Questions"], in *Vospitanie rebionka v sem'e* (Moscow, 1950), p. 230.

3. *Ibid.*, pp. 225–226.

4. A. S. Makarenko, *Polovoe vospitanie [Sex Education]*, in *Sochineniia [Works]* (Moscow, 1951), IV, 410–412. This was one of the strongest convictions of Anton Sem'enovich [Makarenko], and he often returned to this topic in his discussions with me.

5. A. V. Zaporozhets, "Psikhologiia vospriatia skazki rebionkom-doshkol'nikom" ["The Psychology of the Preschooler's Reaction to the Fairy Tale"], *Doshkol'noe vospitanie,* no. 9 (1948), p. 40.

Chapter III. Children and Their Poetry

1. V. G. Belinsky, *Polnoe sobranie sochinenii [Complete Collected Works]* (Moscow: Izd. Akademii Nauk S.S.S.R., 1954), IV, 88.

2. E. I. Stanchinskaia, *Dnevnik materi. Istoria razvitia sovremionnovo rebionka ot rozhdeniia do 7 let [A Mother's Diary. The History of the Development of a Child from Birth to the Age of Seven]* (Moscow, 1924), p. 100.

3. N. Shchedrin, ed., *M. E. Saltykov—Polnoe sobranie sochinenii [Complete Works of M. E. Saltykov]* (Moscow, 1941), I, 82–83.

4. N. Uspenskii, "Derevenskaia Gazeta" ["The Village Newspaper"], in *Sochineniia [Works]* (Moscow, 1933), I, 271.

5. D. V. Grigorovich, *Skuchnye Liudi [Tiresome People]* in *Polnoe sobranie sochinenii [Complete Collected Works]* (St. Petersburg, 1896), VIII, 32.

Chapter IV. The Sense of Nonsense Verse

1. The word *pereviortyshi* [topsy-turvies] has existed in the [Russian] language for a long time. However, the meaning given to this word in this chapter, as a literary term, has not been ascribed to it formerly.

2. Georgii Vinogradov, *Detskii fol'klor* [*Children's Folklore*] (1925); O. Kapitsa, *Detskii fol'klor* (1928); A. P. Babushkina, *Istoria russkoi detskoi literatury* [*The History of Russian Children's Literature*] (Moscow, 1948), p. 18, among others.

3. A. V. Zaporozhets, "Psikhologiia vospriatia skazki rebionkom-doshkol'nikom" ["The Psychology of the Preschooler's Reaction to the Fairy Tale"], *Doshkol'noe vospitanie*, no. 9 (1948), p. 36.

4. Florence V. Barry, *A Century of Children's Books* (London: Methuen, 1922), p. 4.

5. Blanche E. Weeks, *Literature and the Child* (New York, 1935), p. 78.

6. *The Cambridge History of English Literature*, XI, 369–371.

7. *The Works of John Locke* (London, 1824), VIII, 147.

8. "Mother Goose's Nursery Rhymes," *Tales and Jingles* (London and New York: Frederick Warne & Company).

Chapter V. The Battle for the Fairy Tale

1. V. I. Lenin, *Zakliuchitel'noe slovo po politicheskomu otchetu* [*Summary of a Political Report*], Central Committee of the Russian Communist Party at the 11th Congress, March 28, 1922, *Sochineniia* [*Writings*], XXXIII, 284.

2. See article by Professor V. L. Kirpich in *Reports of the Kiev Political Institute* (1903).

3. The archives of A. S. Makarenko; the quotation is from a book by E. Balabanovich, *A. S. Makarenko* (Moscow, 1951), p. 112.

4. *Na putiakh k novoi shkole* [*Toward a New School*], no. 1 (1924).

5. E. I. Stanchinskaia, *Dnevnik materi. Istoria razvitia sovremionnovo rebionka ot rozhdeniia do 7 let* [*A Mother's Diary. The History of the Development of a Child from Birth to the Age of Seven*] (Moscow, 1924), p. 52.

6. *Ibid.,* p. 66.

7. *Ibid.,* p. 92.

8. *Ibid.,* p. 48.

9. N. I. Gavrilova and M. P. Stakhorskaia, eds., *Dnevnik materi* [*The Diary of a Mother*] (Moscow, 1916), p. 52.

10. John Tindale, "The Role of Fantasy in the Development of Science," as quoted in "Rol' fantazii dlia inzhenerov" ["The Role Fantasy Plays for the Engineer"], in *Reports of the Kiev Political Institute* (1903).

11. K. Marx, *K kritike politicheskoi ekonomii* [*Toward a Criticism of Political Economy*] (Gospolitizdat, 1949), p. 225.

12. E. A. Flerina, Vstupitel'naia stat'a v sbornike *Khudozhestvennoie slovo doshkol'niku* [An introductory article to the *Review of the Literary Language for the Preschool Child*] (Moscow, 1952), p. 8.

13. *Russkie narodnye pesni,* sobrannye P. V. Sheinom [*Russian Folk Songs,* collected by P. V. Shein] (Moscow, 1870), p. 48.

Chapter VI. Conversation with Beginners

1. V. Utkov, "P. P. Ershov," Vstupitel'naia stat'ia k *Kon'ku-gorbunku i drugim stikhotvorenii Ershova* ["P. P. Ershov," an introductory article to *The Little Humpbacked-Horse and Other Poems by Ershov*], in *Biblioteka Poeta* [*The Library of the Poet*] (Leningrad, 1951).

2. M. Kitainik, "Detskii fol'klor i detskaia literatura" ["Children's Folklore and Children's Literature"], *Detskaia literatura,* no. 5 (1940), pp. 12–15.

3. A. Barto, "O stikhakh dlia detei" ["About Verses for Children"], *Literaturnaia Gazeta,* no. 2 (1952).